小经典译丛·民

U0690175

（汉英对照版）

古代的人

［美］亨德里克·威廉·房龙 著　林徽因 译

辽宁人民出版社

ANCIENT MAN

by Hendrik Willem Van Loon
Translated by Lin Huiyin

Ⓛ Liaoning People's Publishing House

图书在版编目（CIP）数据

古代的人 /（美）房龙著；林徽因译. —沈阳：辽宁人民出版社，2017.1（2020.6重印）

（小经典译丛）

ISBN 978-7-205-08645-9

Ⅰ.①古… Ⅱ.①房… ②林… Ⅲ.①长篇小说—美国—现代 Ⅳ.①I712.45

中国版本图书馆CIP数据核字（2016）第166501号

出版发行：**辽宁人民出版社**

　　　　　地址：沈阳市和平区十一纬路25号　邮编：110003

　　　　　电话：024-23284321（邮　购）　024-23284324（发行部）

　　　　　传真：024-23284191（发行部）　024-23284304（办公室）

　　　　　http://www.lnpph.com.cn

印　　刷：山东华立印务有限公司

幅面尺寸：110mm×180mm

印　　张：10.5

字　　数：140千字

出版时间：2017年1月第1版

印刷时间：2020年6月第2次印刷

责任编辑：刘国阳

封面设计：展　志

版式设计：姿　兰

责任校对：耿　珺等

书　　号：ISBN 978-7-205-08645-9

定　　价：29.00元

出版说明

　　纵观中外翻译史，翻译活动与语言的发展密不可分。英语发展的各个重要阶段，翻译都发挥了重要作用，不仅丰富了英语的词汇，又极大地增强了英语的表现力。反观我国，古代的佛经翻译对汉语的用词、句法等均产生了影响。胡适的《白话文学史》中讲到，"维祇难，竺法护，鸠摩罗什诸位大师用朴实平易的白话文体来翻译佛经，但求易晓，不加藻饰，遂造成一种文学新体"。我国 19 世纪中叶起有意识地译介西方的地理、历史、政治、法律、教育的书籍，这些翻译活动大大丰富了汉语中的词汇，很多词汇已经融入日常用语并沿用至今，如"文学""法律""政治""铁路""贸易"等。到了 19 世纪末期和 20 世纪初期，梁启超所倡导的"新文体"对当时的读书人有着相当大的影响，而所谓"新文体"即是融合了浅近文言、翻译输入新名词、叙述自由、不合"古文义法"的文体。"小经典译丛·民国名家名译"所精选的翻译作品，就是在这样的背景下诞生的。无论是徐志摩还是郁达夫，均是从小耳濡目染着"新文体"同时又接受了良好的文言和外文的教育。因而，他们的译文既融合了本人母语写作的诗化、含蓄、连绵的特点，也将欧化的语言带入译文。从他们的译文中足以管窥汉语白话文推演之一斑。20世纪30年代语言学家钱玄同谈及汉语过渡时期，曾说应"用某一外国文字为国文之补助"；论及所选语种，则谈"照现在中国学校情形而论，似乎英文已成习惯，则用英文可也"。故而当时的一些知识分子也在译介域外文学时自觉地通过翻译来"改造"语言，例如周作人所倡导的"直译"等。无论是顺应西文词序不自觉地翻译，还是对汉语白话有意识地"改造"，使这一时期的作品都彰显了独特的语言气质——自由、含蓄、唯美、诗意，虽然不能妄言达到"信、达、雅"之境，却也力求用最精到的用词和与原文灵魂契合的句式，用独具风韵的白话进行表达。这也在某种程度上为这些名家的母语创作提供了借鉴。从徐志摩和郁达夫等人的现代诗和散文作品中，也能见到这种语言"改造"的影子。

尽管在习惯了现代汉语行文的读者看来，这些名家的译文多有机巧、不够平易，甚至有些不通，但如果放在当时的背景之下，就可以客观评价和欣赏这种文风的妙处。另外，民国初期很多地名、人名等尚没有严格的规范译名，尤其在文学翻译里，常见到译者的别具匠心的音译或直译，虽缺少了规范，略有理解障碍，但这种自由也促成了一些精妙的译名诞生，如"翡冷翠"（佛罗伦萨）、"沁芳"（交响乐）这样的灵动传神，恐在今天一定是不合规矩、不合时宜的了。

丛书甄选这一时期名家的译介作品，编排名篇的中英文对照，旨在为喜爱欣赏文学和英文的读者提供中英文对照的素材，从比照原文和译文了解名家甄选原文、推敲译文的良苦用心，近距离感受他们的文化底蕴，并从中体会 19 世纪末 20 世纪初世界新旧交替、风云激荡的大背景下，中国文人的趣味和心境。阅读这套丛书，不仅可以品读双语文学经典，还可借此回溯语言文化一路发展的长河，于浪涛中取这一杯啜饮。

丛书编辑过程中，尽量保留了译著的原状，借此为读者呈现民国初期珍贵的语言面貌。编辑过程中仅对个别生僻词句加注说明，并对译文的形式略有改动，如删去了《古代的人》原译中的部分英文括注，以避免与原文对照功能重复。由于编选时间仓促、水平有限，一定有很多不足与疏漏之处，敬请读者批评指正。

辽宁人民出版社

代　序

　　几个月前，受辽宁人民出版社编辑邀约，为他们精编的一套民国名家经典译丛作序，并收到电子初稿小样。虽执教英文近30年，翻译专业书籍、英美小说、杂文等文字量近200万字，但为学贯中西的大文学家、民国时期精英才俊郁达夫、徐志摩、林徽因等人的译作写序，岂敢？故几番推辞，不敢承约。但手中拥有了这份来自故乡的电子书小样，我如获至宝。在北欧夏日极昼极长的日光里，工作之余，悠闲地坐在斑斓树荫下、湖边草坪上或街边咖啡座里，我先睹为快。捧书细读，重温英汉对译的妙与美，我似乎穿越到了上个世纪二十、三十年代的民国时期，与我少年时起就崇拜的冷峻的郁达夫、才情的徐志摩和美丽的林徽因在方方正正的中文里相遇啦！我在字里行间感受民国时期那股清新的译风，在诗化的素美语言中玩味彼时翻译的乐趣，徜徉在看似信手拈来却也处处机巧的篇章中，时间空间仿佛凝滞在那精读时刻。

年少时，也曾读过英文原著小章节。一路走来，人生中年，在英语语境中深入到久远的原著，伴着波罗的海边的余晖，我再一次理解郁达夫作品《沉沦》与他的译作《幸福的摆》的某种关联。主人公华伦徘徊在理性与感性之间，命运从悲喜转为平和，仿佛那身边大海，时而惊涛拍岸，汹涌澎湃，而后又归于平静安详，不仅抒发感叹：这就是人生啊！

某个晴朗的周末，我在湖边草坪席地而坐，像个12岁的小姑娘般充满好奇地读完了亨德里克·威廉·房龙撰写、林徽因译就的《古代的人》。房龙像个博学的圣诞老人，精巧细致地引领读者走入历史长河，贴切的行文勾画人类进步的面面观。而时年22岁的美丽才女林徽因用她缜密的逻辑，精致的文字，醇熟的译法再现出原著风格。读她的作品如同欣赏她设计的精美建筑，那样灵动，那样飘逸。

徐志摩的诗才人尽皆知，他的字句清新、意境优美和神思飘逸是历来文青们效仿的典范。美慧的英国女作家曼殊斐尔人格的精华给了诗人灵澈，他们惺惺相惜。最适合在一个绵绵细雨的日子，捧一杯咖啡或清茶，读《园会》，品《一杯茶》，看《理想的家庭》之模样。诗人用他如诗般的音律，典雅的人名转译，神奇点睛之笔，重现多位栩栩如生的欧美人物形象，亲切而又陌生，仿佛老上海城隍庙游园会，走来一群曼妙的蔷媚，谈着雨夜的翡冷翠……

　　快生活时代，让我们的思想、思绪慢下来，品读经典，体会文字语言的译介之美。让这译介的"媒"引领我们走入东西方文化的"国际理解"之中吧！

张东辉

（英语教授、维尔纽斯大学

孔子学院中方院长）

于维尔纽斯

2016年7月

序 一

房龙的书，已经我们中国人翻译出来的，在我所晓得的范围以内，只有沈性仁女士译的《人类故事》。现在我的朋友林徽因译的《古代的人》，又在这里与中国的小朋友们见面了。

《人类故事》，我没有看过，可是这一本《古代的人》，因为徽因在翻译的当初，曾经和我商榷过几次，所以我的确是为他看过一遍的。

书的内容，和房龙的作书方法，在他的原序里，就可以看出来：

I am not going to present you with a text-book. Neither will it be a volume of pictures. It will not even be a regular history in the accepted sense of the word.

I shall just take both of you by the hand and

together we shall wander forth to explore the
intricate wilderness of the bygone ages.

　　房龙的这一种方法，实在巧妙不过。干燥无
味的科学常识，经他那么的一写，无论大人小
孩，读他的书的人，都觉得娓娓忘倦了。你一行
一行地读下去，就仿佛是和一位白胡须的老头
儿进了历史博物馆在游览。你看见一件奇怪的东
西，他就告诉你一段故事。说的时候，有这老头
儿的和颜笑貌，有这老头儿的咳嗽声音在内，你
到了读完的时候，就觉得这老头儿不见了，但
心里还想寻着他来，再要他讲些古代的话给你
听听。

　　房龙的笔，有这一种魔力。但这也不是他的
特创，这不过是将文学家的手法，拿来用以讲述
科学而已。

　　这一种方法，古时原是有的，但近来似乎格
外的流行了。像诗人雪莱（Shelley）的传记，有
人在用小说的体裁演写，Abelard 和 Heloise 的故
事，有人在当作现实的事情描摩。可是将这一种

方法，应用到叙述科学上来，从前试过的人，也许过，但是成功的，却只有房龙一个。

Tyn Dall 的讲结晶，Macaulay 的叙历史，都不过是字面雄豪，文章美丽而已，从没有这样的安逸，这样的自在，这样的使你不费力而能得到正确的知识的。像这一种方法，我希望中国的科学家，也能常常应用，可使一般懒惰的中国知识阶级，也能于茶余饭后，得到一点科学常识，好打破他们的天圆地方，运命前定的观念。

最后，我还想说一说徽因的译这一本书的缘故。

去年她失了业，时常跑到我这里来。可怜我当时的状态，也和她一样，所以虽则心里很对她表同情，但事实上却一点儿也不能帮她的忙。有一天下雨的午后，她又来和我默默地对坐了半点钟。我因为没有什么话讲，所以就问她："你近来做点什么事情？"她嗫嚅地说："我想翻译一点书来卖钱。"我又问他："你翻译的是什么书？"她回答说，就是这一本《古代的人》。当时我听了很喜欢，因为她也能做一点可以完全自主，不去摇尾乞怜的事情了。但后来听她一说，"出版的地方还找不着！"我又有点担起心事来了，所以就答应她说："你译好了，我就可以为你出版。"后来经过了半年，她书已译好，但我为她出版的能力，却丧失掉了，所以末了只好为她去介绍给孙福熙。福熙现在又跑走了，她的那本《古代的人》，最后才落到了开明书店的手里。此刻听说书已排就，不日要付印了，我为补报她的屡次的失望起见，就为她做了这一篇序，虽然这序文是不足重轻的。

　　一九二七年，八月廿六，郁达夫于上海。

序　二

　　这已是去年夏天的事了：朋友仁松送了我几本《现代丛书》，其中的一本就是这房龙的《古代的人》。我看了觉得很有趣味，就打算把它译出；但是在已译到了三分之一的时候，我不知怎样终止了我的进行。

　　今年自我失业以后，很觉无聊，便时常去看看朋友们。一日在创造社，达夫问起我近来写了什么来没有。"什么都没有写，连已译了三分之一的《古代的人》也不高兴译下去。"他听了便鼓励我继续着译，并担任把它在创造社出版；我就费了一月的工夫，把它译完了。

　　不幸的人连译了的书也是不幸的，我刚把《古代的人》译毕，达夫正在那时离开了创造社；后经了再三的转折，才落到了锡琛先生的手里：

这可说是一件不幸之中的幸事。

在这书付排的时候，我正在杭州，因此，本书的设计，全劳了景深先生的驾，而且插图中的文字也全由他译出，我特在此提出我对于景深先生的谢意。

末了，我谢谢达夫的鼓励与序文。

徽因 一六,一二,三,上海。[①]

---

① "一六"为民国十六年，即1927年。

目 录

CONTENTS

题　首

致罕斯机与威廉，

　　我的最亲爱的小儿们：

　　你们一个是十二岁，一个是八岁。不久你们便会长大成人。你们要离别家庭，去开创你们自己的生活。我已经想到那一日，踌躇着我能帮助你们些什么。终究我已得了一个观念。最好的指南针是彻底地了解人类的生长和经验。所以我要专替你们写一部特种的历史。

　　现在我拿了我的忠诚的科洛那（Corona，是笔的牌号）五瓶墨水一盒火柴和一束纸，而开始工作着第一集。如其一切顺利，接着还有八集，它们会给你们详述关于最近的六千年来你们所应当知道的事。

　　在你们开始读着以前，让我来释明我所想做的。

　　我不是在赠给你们一册课本。它也不是一卷

画集。它甚至于不是一本历史，如同这两个字通常所含的意义一样。

我只是要手携着你们俩，我们要一起向前漂泊着，到这古代的，奥妙的旷野去探险。

我要指给你们，看神秘的江河，这似乎是没有起源的地方，而且被命定着达不到它终极的目的地。

我要带你们切近着危险的深渊，谨慎地隐藏在层出不穷的快乐的而又迷惑的，痴情之境的下面。

往往我们要离开踏平了的道路，爬上一个孤独而寂寞的山峰，这山峰是高耸于周围的村庄的上面的。

除非我们非常地侥幸，我们有时要困迷于突然而起的稠密的无知之雾中。

我们无论到何处去，应披着人类的同情与了解的热诚的大褂，因为广漠的平原会变成不毛的沙漠——被卷于民众的损害和个人的贪欲的冷酷的狂潮；如非我们善备了来，我们要舍弃了我们的人类的信仰，那是，亲爱的小儿们能对我们的任何人所发生的最坏的事情。

我不愿自命为一个万事精通的向导。无论何时你们一有机会便可以跟别的那先前已经过了这同一路由的旅客们斟酌去。你可以把我的话同他们的观察比较一下，如果这引导你们到一不同的结论时，我决不会恼怒你们的。

以前我从没有训诲过你们。

如今我也不是在训诲你们。

你们知道这世界所盼望于你们的是什么——就是你们要做这共同事业的你们的一份，而且要勇敢、愉快地做它。

如其这些书能帮助你们，那是更好。

以我的全爱，我奉献这些历史于你们，并奉献给那些在生命之途上与你们为伴的男孩们和女孩们。

亨德里克·威廉·房龙

DEDICATION TO
HANSJE AND WILLEM

My Darling Boys,

You are twelve and eight years old. Soon you will be grown up. You will leave home and begin your own lives. I have been thinking about that day, wondering what I could do to help you. At last, I have had an idea. The best compass is a thorough understanding of the growth and the experience of the human race. Why should I not write a special history for you?

So I took my faithful Corona and five bottles of ink and a box of matches and a bale of paper and began to work upon the first volume. If all goes well there will be eight more and they will tell you what you ought to know of the last six thousand years.

But before you start to read let me explain what I

intend to do.

I am not going to present you with a textbook. Neither will it be a volume of pictures. It will not even be a regular history in the accepted sense of the word.

I shall just take both of you by the hand and together we shall wander forth to explore the intricate wilderness of the bygone ages.

I shall show you mysterious rivers which seem to come from nowhere and which are doomed to reach no ultimate destination.

I shall bring you close to dangerous abysses, hidden carefully beneath a thick overgrowth of pleasant but deceiving romance.

Here and there we shall leave the beaten track to scale a solitary and lonely peak, towering high above the surrounding country.

Unless we are very lucky we shall sometimes lose ourselves in a sudden and dense fog of ignorance.

Wherever we go we must carry our warm cloak of human sympathy and understanding for vast tracts of land will prove to be a sterile desert—swept by icy storms of popular prejudice and personal greed and unless we come well prepared we shall forsake our faith in humanity and that, dear boys, would be the worst thing that could happen to any of us.

I shall not pretend to be an infallible guide. Whenever you have a chance, take counsel with other travelers who have passed along the same route before. Compare their observations with mine and if this leads you to different conclusions, I shall certainly not be angry with you.

I have never preached to you in times gone by.

I am not going to preach to you today.

You know what the world expects of you—that you shall do your share of the common task and shall do it bravely and cheerfully.

If these books can help you, so much the better.

And with all my love I dedicate these histories to you and to the boys and girls who shall keep you company on the voyage through life.

HENDRIK WILLEM VAN LOON

一　历史以前的人

哥伦布要四星期多才能从西班牙航行到西印度群岛；反之，我们在如飞的汽船中只要十六小时便能驶过洋面了。

五百年前要三四年才能抄成一本书籍；我们有了活排铅字机和旋转印刷机，只要两天便能印成一本新书了。

我们很知道了些解剖学、化学、矿物学并熟悉了论千种的不同的科学，这些从前的人是连名字都不知道的。

然而在一方面，我们是跟原人一般地蒙然——我们不明白我们从何处来。我们不明白人类如何，为何或何时才进行到这"宇宙"中。我们虽恣意地想遍了千方万法，却依旧只能照着童话的老方法，这样起头：

"从前有一个人。"

这人生在几千百年以前。

他是怎样的相貌呢?

我们不知道。我们从没见过他的图像。有时候我们从深的古代的泥土中寻见他的几块骨骸来。它们搀和在早已绝迹于这地球的动物的骨骸中。我们用这些骨骸来重构成这曾做过我们祖先的奇异的形象。

人类的始祖是一种很丑陋而不动人的哺乳动物。他是十分地小。太阳的热光和冬日的烈风使他的皮肤转为深褐色。他的头和肢体的大部分都被长的毛发覆盖着。他的手好像猴子的手指很细,但很有力。他的前额是低的。他的牙床是像野兽的牙床一般,用牙齿如用刀叉。

他不穿衣服。除了以它们的烟和容石充满了这地球的隆隆的火山之焰外,他看不见火。

他住在潮湿而黑暗的深林中。

当饥饿的痛苦袭来时,他便吃植物的生叶和生根,或者从凶狠的鸟的窠内偷蛋。

有时,经过了长时间的耐心的追逐后,才好容易得到了一只麻雀或一只小野狗或一只兔子。这些他都是生吃的,因历史以前的人,还不知道食物可以煮来吃呢。

他的牙齿是大的，正像现在有几种动物的牙齿一般。

当白天时，这原人出去为他自己，为他的妻子并为他的子女找寻食物。

晚上呢，他听见了出来寻食的野兽可怕声音，便爬进一株空树中，或者藏在青苔和大蜘蛛的几块大石后面。

夏日他赤裸着受太阳光的焦灼。冬日他受严寒。

他受了伤时，并没有人来看护他，而且打猎是始终会折伤了他们的骨头，或扭转了他们的踝节的。

遇危险时，他会喊出一种警告他同族人的声音，这正像狗见了陌生人会叫一样。在好几方面，他还远不如一只养家的小狗或小猫动人。

总之，古人是很可怜的，他住在惊恐和饥饿的时代，他周围是论千的仇敌，他是永远被

有史以前的人

亲朋的幽灵作祟着，那些亲朋是已被狼熊或齿利如刀的虎所吞食了的。

关于这人的最初的历史，我们一些都不知道。他没有器具，也不盖屋。他生了死了，并不留一点他曾经存在的痕迹。从他的骨殖，我们才追知他是生在二千世纪以前。其余的是蒙昧不明。

直到了有名的"石器时代"，人才学得了我们所谓文化的初步原理。

关于这石器时代，我得详细地告诉你们。

I. PREHISTORIC MAN

IT took Columbus more than four weeks to sail from Spain to the West Indian Islands. We on the other hand cross the ocean in sixteen hours in a flying machine.

Five hundred years ago, three or four years were necessary to copy a book by hand. We possess linotype machines and rotary presses and we can print a new book in a couple of days.

We understand a great deal about anatomy and chemistry and mineralogy and we are familiar with a thousand different branches of science of which the very name was unknown to the people of the past.

In one respect, however, we are quite as ignorant as the most primitive of men—we do not know where we came from. We do not know how or why or when the human race began its career upon this

Earth. With a million facts at our disposal we are still obliged to follow the example of the fairy-stories and begin in the old way:

"Once upon a time there was a man."

This man lived hundreds of thousands of years ago.

What did he look like?

We do not know. We never saw his picture. Deep in the clay of an ancient soil we have sometimes found a few pieces of his skeleton. They were hidden amidst masses of bones of animals that have long since disappeared from the face of the earth. We have taken these bones and they allow us to reconstruct the strange creature who happens to be our ancestor.

The great-great-grandfather of the human race was a very ugly and unattractive mammal. He was quite small. The heat of the sun and the biting wind of the cold winter had colored his skin a dark brown. His head and most of his body were covered with long hair. He had very thin but strong fingers which made his hands look like those of a monkey. His forehead was low and his jaw was like the jaw of a wild animal which uses its teeth both as fork and knife.

He wore no clothes. He had seen no fire except the flames of the rumbling volcanoes which filled the earth with their smoke and their lava.

He lived in the damp blackness of vast forests.

When he felt the pangs of hunger he ate raw leaves and the roots of plants or he stole the eggs from the nest of an angry bird.

Once in a while, after a long and patient chase, he managed to catch a sparrow or a small wild dog or perhaps a rabbit. These he would eat raw, for prehistoric man did not know that food could be cooked.

His teeth were large and looked like the teeth of many of our own animals.

During the hours of day this primitive human being went about in search of food for himself and his wife and his young.

At night, frightened by the noise of the beasts,

who were in search of prey, he would creep into a hollow tree or he would hide himself behind a few big boulders, covered with moss and great, big spiders.

In summer he was exposed to the scorching rays of the sun.

During the winter he froze with cold.

When he hurt himself (and hunting animals are for ever breaking their bones or spraining their ankles) he had no one to take care of him.

He had learned how to make certain sounds to warn his fellow-beings whenever danger threatened. In this he resembled a dog who barks when a stranger approaches. In many other respects he was far less attractive than a well-bred house pet.

Altogether, early man was a miserable creature who lived in a world of fright and hunger, who was surrounded by a thousand enemies and who was for ever haunted by the vision of friends and relatives who had been eaten up by wolves and bears and the terrible sabre-toothed tiger.

Of the earliest history of this man we know nothing. He had no tools and he built no homes. He lived and died and left no traces of his existence. We keep track of him through his bones and they tell us that he lived more than two thousand centuries ago.

The rest is darkness.

Until we reach the time of the famous Stone Age, when man learned the first rudimentary principles of what we call civilization.

Of this Stone Age I must tell you in some detail.

二　宇宙渐渐地冷了

气候有所变化。

古人并不知"时间"是什么。

生日，结婚纪念或死期于他全无记录。

日子，星期或年岁于他毫无概念。

当早上太阳升起时，他并不说"又是一天"。他说"这是'光'"。他便利用了这朝日的光线去为他的一家采集食物。

天在渐渐地暗的时候，他回去，把他白天所得到的一部分（大概是些浆果和几只鸟雀）给他的妻子和小孩。他自己呢，吃饱了生肉便去睡觉。

他从长期的经验而知道了季候的变迁，寒冷的冬天过了，便照例地来了温和的春天，春天老去，便是炎热的夏天，那时果子也成熟了，稻麦等的穗也可采食了。夏天一过，暴风便来吹落树上的叶子，并且有些动物便爬进洞去过那长期的蛰伏。

季候老是这样变迁着。古人领悟了这些有用的寒来暑往的变迁，可是并不发生疑问他活着，那便很够使他满足了。

冰结的时代

然而，骤然有很使他烦扰的事情发生了。

炎热的夏天来得很迟。果子一些也不成熟。本来常被青草覆盖着的山顶，现在却深藏在一层厚厚的雪的底下了。

一日早晨，有一大群跟他山谷中的居民不同的野人，从高山上来了。

他们所说的话，没有一个人能够懂得。他们貌似瘦瘠而面现饥容。他们似乎被饥寒所迫，而离了他们的老家。

这谷中的食物，不足供给新来旧在的两民族。他们想久居时，便发生了一场惊人的争斗，而全民族都被杀死了。其余的人便逃入了森林，以后也没有再见过。

好久好久并没有稍微重要的事情发生。

不过，老是日渐渐地短而夜较平时为冷。

后来，在两高山之罅窍间，显现了一小块微绿的冰块。这冰块日积月累地涨大。一条庞大的冰川很慢地从山坡上滚下来，大石块被冲入溪谷中。在惊天动地的声音中，大石块忽然从惊吓着的人民中滚过，而将正睡着的他们压死了。百年的大树被墙般高的冰块挤得粉碎，这无论对于人或兽是一般地没有怜恤之情。

终究，下雪了。

雪是整月整月地下着。

一切的植物全死了。动物奔就南方的太阳。这山谷便成了不能再居人的场所。人背了他的子女，带了几件用作利器的石片前去另觅新家。

穴居人

我们不明白为甚这宇宙到了某一时期必得变冷。我们连那缘由都揣摩不出。

然而，气候的渐低，使人类起了一个重大的

变化。

有一时，人类似乎要死得一个都不留。但是，结果，这气候的变化反造福于人类。气候杀尽了弱者的全体，使余生者为继续保存生命起见，不得不发展他们的智能。

临到了不能沉思便须速死的当儿，即用那前曾从石片做成斧头的脑筋，现在解决了些上代人从不曾想到过的困难问题。

第一步，来了穿衣的问题。若不借人工的遮蔽物，这简直会冷得受不住。在北极的熊、野牛和别的野兽身上，都有一层厚厚的毛以御冰雪之寒。人却没有这种类似的御寒物。他的皮肤是很柔弱的，而遭遇的却颇严酷。

他用了很简便的法子解决了他的穿衣问题。他掘了一个地洞，用枝叶小草等覆盖着。熊走来的时候，便跌入这人工的地穴中。他等到它饿得疲乏时，便用大石击死它。他用块锋利的火石从它的背上割下了它的毛皮。于是他把它在稀疏的日光下曝干了，披在肩上，以享受熊曾享受过的幸福而安适的温暖。

其次，是住屋的问题。有许多动物是惯于

睡在黑暗的洞中的。人也照样寻到了一个空洞。他跟蝙蝠和各种爬虫类住在一起，毫不介意。只要他的新屋能够使他得到温暖，他就满足了。

起雷阵的时候，时常树枝被电击倒了。有时全森林着了火，人看见过这些燎原之火，他走得太近时，便会被热气所冲去。现在他记起了火能生热。

本来，火老是做着人的仇敌的，现在却成为朋友了。

把枯树拖进洞来，再从着火的树林里取出尚未熄灭的树枝，拿回来引燃枯树，屋中便满布着特异而快适的热气。

也许你要笑，这些似乎全是很简易的事情。我们之所以把它们看成很简易，就是因为有人在许多许多年以前，用他的聪明早已想明了的缘故。然而当第一个洞中安适地用枯树引火时，比第一家人家用电灯时，更来得引人注意。

在后来有一特殊伶俐的人，偶得了将生肉掷在火灰中煨了吃的观念时，在人类知识的总和上

他已加上了一分，这使穴居的人觉得已到了文化
的顶点。

如今我们听到又一惊异的发明时，我们是很
骄傲的。

"人的悟性，还能更有所成就吗？"我们问。

我们满意地笑，因为我们住在这超凡的时期
内，从没人有过如我们的工程师和化学家所成就
的如此的奇事。

在四万年前，这宇宙还在冻得死人的时代，
有一不栉不沐的穴居的人（用他的褐色的手指和
他的大而白的牙齿，旋去一只半死了的小鸡的
毛——将毛和骨随地弃了做他和他的全家人的
床褥的），学得了怎样生肉会从火之余烬中变成
可口的食物时，也会觉得一样的快乐，一样的
骄傲。

"怎样可惊异的年代呀。"他会说。他会躺在
他那当饭粮吃了的动物的腐烂的骨骼中，而幻想
他自己的完满，那时小狗般大的蝙蝠不息地飞过
洞穴，小猫般大的耗子从废堆中搜寻余粒。

那是常有的事，山洞被四围的岩石压坍了。
于是人也搀和在亲自为他牺牲的动物的骨头中。

　　数千年后，人类学家（问你的父亲，那是什么意思）带了他的小铲和独轮车来了。

　　他掘，掘，掘，终究掘出了这幕陈旧的悲剧，由此，我也可告诉你们关于它的一切。

II. THE WORLD GROWS COLD

SOMETHING was the matter with the weather.

Early man did not know what "time" meant.

He kept no records of birthdays and wedding-anniversaries or the hour of death.

He had no idea of days or weeks or years.

When the sun arose in the morning he did not say "Behold another day". He said "It is Light" and he used the rays of the early sun to gather food for his family.

When it grew dark, he returned to his wife and children, gave them part of the day's catch (some berries and a few birds), stuffed himself full with raw meat and went to sleep.

In a very general way he kept track of the seasons.

Long experience had taught him that the cold Winter was invariably followed by the mild Spring—that Spring grew into the hot Summer when fruits ripened and the wild ears of corn were ready to be plucked and eaten. The Summer ended when gusts of wind swept the leaves from the trees and when a number of animals crept into their holes to make ready for the long hibernal sleep.

It had always been that way. Early man accepted these useful changes of cold and warm but asked no questions. He lived and that was enough to satisfy him.

Suddenly, however, something happened that worried him greatly.

The warm days of Summer had come very late. The fruits had not ripened at all. The tops of the mountains which used to be covered with grass lay deeply hidden under a heavy burden of snow.

Then one morning quite a number of wild people, different from the other inhabitants of his valley had approached from the region of the high peaks.

They muttered sounds which no one could understand. They looked lean and appeared to be starving. Hunger and cold seemed to have driven them from their former homes.

There was not enough food in the valley for both the old inhabitants and the newcomers. When they tried to stay more than a few days there was a terrible fight and whole families were killed. The others fled into the woods and were not seen again.

For a long time nothing occurred of any importance.

But all the while, the days grew shorter and the nights were colder than they ought to have been.

Finally, in a gap between the two high hills, there appeared a tiny speck of greenish ice. It increased in size as the years went by. Very slowly a gigantic glacier was sliding down the slopes of the mountain ridge. Huge stones were being pushed into the valley. With the noise of a dozen thunderstorms they suddenly tumbled among the frightened people and killed them while they slept. Century-old trees were crushed into kindling wood by the high walls of ice that knew of no mercy to either man or beast.

At last, it began to snow.

It snowed for months and months and months.

All the plants died. The animals fled in search of the southern sun. The valley became uninhabitable. Man hoisted his children upon his back, took the few pieces of stone which he had used as a weapon and went forth to find a new home.

Why the world should have grown cold at that particular moment, we do not know. We can not even guess at the cause.

The gradual lowering of the temperature, however, made a great difference to the human race.

For a time it looked as if every one would die. But in the end this period of suffering proved a real blessing. It killed all the weaker people and forced the survivors to sharpen their wits lest they perish, too.

Placed before the choice of hard thinking or quick dying the same brain that had first turned a stone into a hatchet now solved difficulties which had never faced the older generations.

In the first place, there was the question of clothing. It had grown much too cold to do without some sort of artificial covering. Bears and bisons and other animals who live in northern regions are protected against snow and ice by a heavy coat of fur. Man possessed no such coat. His skin was very delicate and he suffered greatly.

He solved his problem in a very simple fashion. He dug a hole and he covered it with branches and leaves and a little grass. A bear came by and fell into this artificial cave. Man waited until the creature was weak from lack of food and then killed him with many blows of a big stone. With a sharp piece of flint he cut the fur of the animal's back. Then he dried it in the sparse rays of the sun, put it around his own shoulders and enjoyed the same warmth that had formerly kept the bear happy and comfortable.

Then there was the housing problem. Many animals were in the habit of sleeping in a dark cave. Man followed their example and searched until he found an empty grotto. He shared it with bats and all sorts of creeping insects but this he did not mind. His new home kept him warm and that was enough.

Often, during a thunderstorm a tree had been hit by lightning. Sometimes the entire forest had been set on fire. Man had seen these forest-fires. When he had come too near he had been driven away by the heat. He now remembered that fire gave warmth.

Thus far, fire had been an enemy.

Now it became a friend.

A dead tree, dragged into a cave and lighted by means of smouldering branches from a burning forest filled the room with unusual but very pleasant heat.

Perhaps you will laugh. All these things seem so very simple. They are very simple to us because some one, ages and ages ago, was clever enough to think of them. But the first cave that was made comfortable by the fire of an old log attracted more attention than the first house that ever was lighted by electricity.

When at last, a specially brilliant fellow hit upon the idea of throwing raw meat into the hot ashes before eating it, he added something to the sum total of human knowledge which made the cave-man feel that the height of civilization had been reached.

Nowadays, when we hear of another marvelous invention we are very proud.

"What 's more," we ask, "can the human brain accomplish?"

And we smile contentedly for we live in the most remarkable of all ages and no one has ever performed such miracles as our engineers and our chemists.

Forty thousand years ago when the world was on the point of freezing to death, an unkempt and unwashed caveman, pulling the feathers out of a half-dead chicken with the help of his brown fingers and his big white teeth—throwing the feathers and the bones upon the same floor that served him and his family as a bed, felt just as happy and just as proud when he was taught how the hot cinders of a fire would change raw meat into a delicious meal.

"What a wonderful age," he would exclaim and he would lie down amidst the decaying skeletons of the animals which had served him as his dinner and he would dream of his own perfection while bats, as large as small dogs, flew restlessly through the cave and while rats, as big as small cats, rummaged among the leftovers.

Quite often the cave gave way to the pressure of the surrounding rock. Then man was hurled amidst the bones of his own victims.

Thousands of years later the anthropologist (ask your father what that means) comes along with his little spade and his wheelbarrow.

He digs and he digs and at last he uncovers this age-old tragedy and makes it possible for me to tell you all about it.

三　石器时代的终了

在严寒期，为生存的挣扎是可惊的。有好几种人和动物，我们寻到了他们的骨头的，可是，在这地球上，已绝了他们的踪迹。

全种族均被饥寒与缺乏所抹去。年幼的先死，继而年长的也死。古代的人是听命于那赶速来占据这无可防护的山洞的野兽。直到气候又改变了，或者空气中的湿度渐低，致使那些野性的侵占者不可再生存时，他们便被逼的退住到阿非利加丛林中去，至今他们还是住在那儿。

因为那些我所一定要叙述的变迁，是这样地迟迟的，这样地渐渐的，我的这一部分的历史，便很不容易写了。

自然是永不急躁的。她有成就她事业的无穷的时间，她能以深思熟虑供给于必要的变迁。

当冰块远降于山谷之下而散布在大部的欧罗巴大陆上时，历史以前的人至少已生存过四个明确的时代。

大约在三万年前，其中的末一时代到了它的终点。

从那时以后，人留给了我们器具、兵器和图像以证明他确然存在过，而且，我们大概可以说历史开端了，当末了的一个严寒时代成为过去的事实时。

为生存的无穷的竞争，给了余生者以许多的知识。

当时的石器和木器，如我们今日的铁器一般地通行。

拙笨的碎片的火石斧，渐渐地变成更切实用的磨光的火石了。人用了这可袭击那自始便给制伏着的许多动物。

庞大的象不再见了。

麝牛退居于南、北极去了。

老虎到底离开了欧罗巴。

穴居的熊不再食小孩了。

一切生物中最柔弱而最无助的"人"，用了他强有力的脑筋，造出了如此可怕的破坏器，他现在成了动物界的领袖了。

对于"自然"的第一次伟大的胜利已经得到，但是其余的不久便也继续着。

完备了渔猎的两种器具，穴居的人便去寻觅新居留地了。

湖边河沿是最容易得到日用粮食的地方。

人类舍弃了旧穴而移向水边去了。

现在人能执了重重的斧头不很费事地将树砍下来了。

鸟类不断地用木片和青草在树枝中造成它们安适的窠。

人抄袭了它们的成法。

他也为他自己造了一窠而叫它做"家"。

除了亚细亚的一小部分外，他并不附着树枝造，那里他嫌太小些，并且生活也不安全。

他砍下了许多木材，将这些木材密密地推下柔滑的浅湖的底下去。在那些上面，他筑一座木头的平台，在平台上面，盖他的破天荒的木屋。

这使他得到了较旧穴更多的利益。

没有野兽和劫夺者能够侵入这屋子了。湖的本身便是一间用不尽的贮藏室，那里供给着无穷的鲜鱼。

　　这些造在桩上的屋子，比旧穴要坚固得多，而且小孩也由此得到了一个长成健全的人的机会。人口稳定地增长着，从没被占据过的广阔的旷野，人也开始去占据了。

　　与时俱进的新发明，使得生命更安适而少危险。

　　实在，这些革新，不是借了人的聪明的脑筋。

　　他仅仅抄袭了动物。

　　你们自然知道有很多的兽类，当物产丰富的夏天，收藏了许多坚果，橡实和别种食物以备长冬之需。只要看松鼠，它永远为冬季和早春在它园中的储藏室内预备着食品，就可以明白了。

　　有些地方知识还不如松鼠的古人，还不知怎样为将来预存些东西。

　　他吃饱了便任凭那些剩余的东西腐烂掉，因为当时他不需要它，结果，到了寒天，他时常得不到他的食物，因此，他的大多部分的小孩便死于饥饿和缺乏之中了。

　　后来他学了动物的样子，当收获正盛，谷麦正多的时候，收藏得很丰富，以备将来之用。

　　我们不知道哪一个天才创始用陶器，然而他是应得建像的。

　　大概的情形是这样的，有一女子做倦了她日常的厨下的工作，打算对她的家政稍微弄出一些条理来。她注意到暴露在日光之下的泥块会炙成坚硬的质地。

　　如一块平的泥会变成一块砖瓦，那么，一块微凹的泥也一定会变成一件微凹的东西。

　　注意，砖瓦变成了陶器时人类便能为明天保存食物了。

　　如果你以为我赞美陶器的发明是夸大的，你就留心你晨餐桌上的陶器（有各式各样的），看它在你的生活中有怎样的意义。

　　你的雀麦面是用盆子盛着。

　　乳酪是用瓶子装着。

　　你的鸡子是放在碟子内，从厨房里送到你的餐室的桌子上。

　　你的牛乳是倒在有柄的瓷杯内送给你。

　　再到贮藏室去（如果你家里没有贮藏室，到最近的一家熟食铺去），你会看见各种食物，也许明天就得吃着的，也许要到下星期或明年才得吃着的，都放在缸内、瓶内、杯内和别种人造的容器内，那些"自然"并没有为我们设备，只好由人发明而完成之，因为那样才可以一年到头无乏食之虞。

就是一个煤气池，也不过是一只大缸，所以用铁做者，因为铁没有瓷般容易碎，没有黏土般多微隙。桶、瓶、壶、罐等也是如此。它们都是同样地用来给我们为将来保存现时所多着的食物。

因它能为他日的需要而预存可吃的东西，人才种了菜蔬和五谷，余下的保存了以备将来之消用。

这可解明了为甚我们从石器时代的后期，寻到了最初辟成的麦田和菜园，群集在先前的桩上居民的居留地的周围。

这也可使我们明白为甚人结束了他的漂泊的生活而占着一固定的地点，在那里生着他的子女，直到死了，便合适地葬在他本族的中间。

这是可信的，如果我们这些最初的祖先能继续活着，他们定会随意地脱出了他们的野蛮。

然而骤然地一个终期隔离了他们。

历史以前的人是发现了。

有一个从无穷的南方来的旅客，勇敢地经过了狂暴的海和险峻的山路而达到了野人聚居的中欧罗巴。

有史以前人类之发现

在他的背上他负了一个包。

他展开他的物品在土人面前。土人们一看，不觉张口结舌，惊诧不已，他们的眼不转睛地注视着，这些奇怪东西是他们连梦想都从不敢梦想的。

他们看见古铜的锤和斧，铁制的器具，铜制的盔和美丽的饰物等，其中有一种是五颜六色的东西，那从外国来的人称这东西为"玻璃"。

当夜石器时代便到了它的终极。

一个新进的文化来补充了，它掷弃了几世纪来的木石的器具，而埋下了那"铁器时代"的基础，这至今还是持续着。

此后我要在此书中对你们详述的就是关于这

新文化；而且如你们不介意，我们要将北大陆搁置二千年而一访埃及和西亚细亚。

"然而，"你要说，"这是不公允。你应许我们讲解历史以前的人的，可是才在感到那故事的兴趣时，你便结束了那一章而跳到世界的别一部去了，而且，不管我们的喜欢不喜欢，也得跟着你跳。"

我知道，这似乎做的不大对。

不幸地，历史绝不跟数学相同。

你解答数学习题时，你是从子到丑，从丑到寅，从寅到卯……按步就班地做去。

历史是恰恰相反，与整洁和秩序是毫不相关的。从子跳到亥，然后跳回到寅，接着再跳到申。

这有一个完满的理由。

历史并不就是精密的科学。

历史是讲到人类的故事的，虽然我们颇想改变他们的天性，他们总不能照着九九表般整齐而精密的行为的。

从没两个人丝毫不错地做过同样的事情。

从没有两个人的思想确切地达到同样的

结论。

你长大起来时，你自己会观察得到。

几百世纪以前的情形并不两样。

我刚对你们说过，历史以前的人是在一步一步地进步着的。

他为活着，曾处治了冰雪和野兽，而且那些本来是很多的。

他曾发明了不少的有用的东西。

然而，那世界的别一部人突然进了这族来。

他们向前猛进得惊人，在一个很短促的时期内，他们达到了文化的最高点，这是在这地球上以前所从没发现过的文化。于是以他们所知道的去教导那些知识不如他们的人。

现在我已将这些对你们解释明白了，这不是似乎此书的每一章全该被埃及人和西亚细亚人所占去么？

III. THE END
OF THE STONE AGE

THE struggle to keep alive during the cold period was terrible. Many races of men and animals, whose bones we have found, disappeared from the face of the earth.

Whole tribes and clans were wiped out by hunger and cold and want. First the children would die and then the parents. The old people were left to the mercy of the wild animals who hastened to occupy the undefended cave. Until another change in the climate or the slowly decreasing moisture of the air made life impossible for these wild invaders and forced them to find a retreat in the heart of the African jungle where they have lived ever since.

This part of my history is very difficult because the changes which I must describe were so very slow and so very gradual.

Nature is never in a hurry. She has all eternity in which to accomplish her task and she can afford to bring about the necessary changes with deliberate care.

Prehistoric man lived through at least four definite eras when the ice descended far down into the valleys and covered the greater part of the European continent.

The last one of these periods came to an end almost thirty thousand years ago.

From that moment on man left behind him concrete evidence of his existence in the form of tools and arms and pictures and in a general way we can say that history begins when the last cold period had become a thing of the past.

The endless struggle for life had taught the survivors many things.

Stone and wooden implements had become as common as steel tools are in our own days.

Gradually the rudely chipped flint axe had

been replaced by one of polished flint which was infinitely more practical. It allowed man to attack many animals at whose mercy he had been since the beginning of time.

The mammoth was no longer seen.

The musk-ox had retreated to the polar circle.

The tiger had left Europe for good.

The cave-bear no longer ate little children.

The powerful brain of the weakest and most helpless of all living creatures—Man—had devised such terrible instruments of destruction that he was now the master of all the other animals.

The first great victory over Nature had been gained but many others were to follow.

Equipped with a full set of tools both for hunting and fishing, the cave-dweller looked for new living quarters.

The shores of rivers and lakes offered the best opportunity for a regular livelihood.

The old caves were deserted and the human race moved toward the water.

Now that man could handle heavy axes, the felling of trees no longer offered any great difficulties.

For countless ages birds had been constructing comfortable houses out of chips of wood and grass amidst the branches of trees.

Man followed their example.

He, too, built himself a nest and called it his "home".

He did not, except in a few parts of Asia, take to the trees which were a bit too small and unsteady for his purpose.

He cut down a number of logs. These he drove firmly into the soft bottom of a shallow lake. On top of them he constructed a wooden platform and upon this platform he erected his first wooden house.

It offered many advantages over the old cave.

No wild animals could break into it and robbers could not enter it. The lake itself was an inexhaustible store-room containing an endless supply of fresh fish.

These houses built on piles were much healthier

than the old caves and they gave the children a chance to grow up into strong men. The population increased steadily and man began to occupy vast tracts of wilderness which had been unoccupied since the beginning of time.

And all the time new inventions were made which made life more comfortable and less dangerous.

Often enough these innovations were not due to the cleverness of man's brain.

He simply copied the animals.

You know of course that there are a large number of beasties who prepare for the long winter by burying nuts and acorns and other food which is abundant during the summer. Just think of the squirrels who are for ever filling their larder in gardens and parks with supplies for the winter and the early spring.

Early man, less intelligent in many respects than the squirrels, had not known how to preserve anything for the future.

He ate until his hunger was stilled, but what he

did not need right away he allowed to rot. As a result he often went without his meals during the cold period and many of his children died from hunger and want.

Until he followed the example of the animals and prepared for the future by laying in sufficient stores when the harvest had been good and there was an abundance of wheat and grain.

We do not know which genius first discovered the use of pottery but he deserves a statue.

Very likely it was a woman who had got tired of the eternal chores of the kitchen and wanted to make her household duties a little less exacting. She noticed that chunks of clay, when exposed to the rays of the sun, got baked into a hard substance.

If a flat piece of clay could be transformed into a brick, a slightly curved piece of the same material must produce a similar result.

And behold, the brick grew into a piece of pottery and the human race was able to save for the day of tomorrow.

If you think that my praises of this invention are exaggerated, look at the breakfast table and see what pottery, in one form and the other, means in your own life.

Your oatmeal is served in a dish.

The cream is served from a pitcher.

Your eggs are carried from the kitchen to the dining-room table on a plate.

Your milk is brought to you in a china mug. Then go to the store-room (if there is no store-room in your house go to the nearest Delicatessen store). You will see how all the things which we are supposed to eat tomorrow and next week and next year have been put away in jars and cans and other artificial containers which Nature did not provide for us but which man was forced to invent and perfect before he could be assured of his regular meals all the year around.

Even a gas-tank is nothing but a large pitcher, made of iron because iron does not break as easily as china and is less porous than clay. So are barrels and bottles and pots and pans. They all serve the same purpose—of providing us in the future with those things of which we happen to have an abundance at the present moment.

And because he could preserve eatable things for the day of need, man began to raise vegetables and grain and saved the surplus for future consumption.

This explains why, during the late Stone Age, we find the first wheat-fields and the first gardens, grouped around the settlements of the early pile-dwellers.

It also tells us why man gave up his habit of wandering and settled down in one fixed spot where he raised his children until the day of his death when he was decently buried among his own people.

It is safe to say that these earliest ancestors of ours would have given up the ways of savages of their own accord if they had been left to their fate.

But suddenly there was an end to their isolation.

Prehistoric man was discovered.

A traveler from the unknown south-land who had

dared to cross the turbulent sea and the forbidding mountain passes had found his way to the wild people of Central Europe.

On his back he carried a pack.

When he had spread his wares before the gaping curiosity of the bewildered natives, their eyes beheld wonders of which their minds had never dared to dream.

They saw bronze hammers and axes and tools made of iron and helmets made of copper and beautiful ornaments consisting of a strangely colored substance which the foreign visitor called "glass".

And overnight the Age of Stone came to an end.

It was replaced by a new civilization which had discarded wooden and stone implements centuries before and had laid the foundations for that "Age of Metal" which has endured until our own day.

It is of this new civilization that I shall tell you in the rest of my book and if you do not mind, we shall leave the northern continent for a couple of thousand years and pay a visit to Egypt and to western Asia.

"But," you will say, "this is not fair. You promise to tell us about prehistoric man and then, just when the story is going to be interesting, you close the chapter and you jump to another part of the world and we must jump with you whether we like it or not."

I know. It does not seem the right thing to do.

Unfortunately, history is not at all like mathematics.

When you solve a sum you go from "a" to "b" and from "b" to "c" and from "c" to "d" and so on.

History on the other hand jumps from "a" to "z" and then back to "f" and next to "m" without any apparent respect for neatness and order.

There is a good reason for this.

History is not exactly a science.

It tells the story of the human race and most people, however much we may try to change their nature, refuse to behave with the regularity and the precision of the tables of multiplication.

No two men ever do precisely the same thing.

No two human brains ever reach exactly the same

conclusion.

You will notice that for yourself when you grow up.

It was not different a few hundred centuries ago.

Prehistoric man, as I just told you, was on a fair way to progress.

He had managed to survive the ice and the snow and the wild animals and that in itself, was a great deal.

He had invented many useful things.

Suddenly, however, other people in a different part of the world entered the race.

They rushed forward at a terrible speed and within a very short space of time they reached a height of civilization which had never before been seen upon our planet. Then they set forth to teach what they knew to the others who had been less intelligent than themselves.

Now that I have explained this to you, does it not seem just to give the Egyptians and the people of western Asia their full share of the chapters of this book?

四　人类之最初的学校

我们是实用时代的骄子。

我们坐在小的自动的我们叫它做汽车的里面，从这里旅行到那里。

我们要对住在千哩（英里旧也作哩）以外的朋友谈话时，我们便对橡皮管"哈罗"一声，并报了一个在芝加哥的德律风的某一个号数。

夜了，房间内渐现黑暗时，我们一扭机括便有光了。

如其我们觉到冷时，我们再扭另一机括，我们的书室内便布满了电汽火炉所发出的温适的光热。

反之，在炎热的夏天时，那同样的电流会鼓动成一种细微的人工的风波（就是电扇），使得我们凉爽而舒适。

我们好像是各种自然力的主人，我们役使它们如同很忠诚的奴隶般，为我们做事。

不过，在你夸诩我们的显赫的事业时，不要忘记了一件事。

我们在古代的人经了千辛万苦所筑成的聪明的基础上，建造着我们的近代文化的大厦。

以下数章，每页上会见到的他们古怪的名字，请你们不要惊诧。

巴比伦人、埃及人、加尔底亚人和萨马利亚人是全已死去了，然而，他们依旧影响着我们生活中的每一件事：我们写的文字，我们用的言语，我们在造一座桥或建一幢高厦大屋之前，所必须解答的复杂的算题。

他们应得我们的怀念的敬意，直到这地球停止了在宇宙的广空中旋转为止。

现在我要对你们讲，这些古代的人民，是分住在三处的。

其中的二处，是建设在广阔的江河之两岸。

第三处位于地中海之滨。

最初的文化中心，发展于埃及的尼罗河流域。

第二个是在西亚细亚的二大河之间的肥沃的平原上，古代人给它起一个名字，叫作美索不达迷亚。

第三个你会沿地中海之滨找到，那里居住着腓尼基人，——全侨民之中最早者，还居住着犹太人，他们以他们的道德律的基本原理给予世界的其余部分。

第三个文化的中心，照古代的巴比伦的名字叫苏立，或者，照我们的发音是叙利亚。

生在这些区域内的人民的历史有五千余年。

这是节复杂而又复杂的历史。

我不能对你们讲解得十分详细。

我要试将他们所经历的事迹编成一件织物，它会像你读过的瑟希辣最德讲给公正的哈纶听的故事中的使人惊异的毛毡之一张。

IV. THE EARLIEST SCHOOL
OF THE HUMAN RACE

WE are the children of a practical age.
We travel from place to place in our
own little locomotives which we call automobiles.

When we wish to speak to a friend whose home
is a thousand miles away, we say "Hello" into a
rubber tube and ask for a certain telephone number
in Chicago.

At night when the room grows dark we push a
button and there is light.

If we happen to be cold we push another button
and the electric stove spreads its pleasant glow
through our study.

On the other hand in summer when it is hot the
same electric current will start a small artificial
storm (an electric fan) which keeps us cool and

comfortable.

We seem to be the masters of all the forces of nature and we make them work for us as if they were our very obedient slaves.

But do not forget one thing when you pride yourself upon our splendid achievements.

We have constructed the edifice of our modern civilization upon the fundament of wisdom that had been built at great pains by the people of the ancient world.

Do not be afraid of their strange names which you will meet upon every page of the coming chapters.

Babylonians and Egyptians and Chaldeans and Sumerians are all dead and gone, but they continue to influence our own lives in everything we do, in the letters we write, in the language we use, in the complicated mathematical problems which we must solve before we can build a bridge or a skyscraper.

And they deserve our grateful respect as long as our planet continues to race through the wide space of the high heavens.

These ancient people of whom I shall now tell you lived in three definite spots.

Two of these were found along the banks of vast rivers.

The third was situated on the shores of the Mediterranean.

The oldest center of civilization developed in the valley of the Nile, in a country which was called Egypt.

The second was located in the fertile plains between two big rivers of western Asia, to which the ancients gave the name of Mesopotamia.

The third one which you will find along the shore of the Mediterranean, was inhabited by the Phoenicians, the earliest of all colonizers and by the Jews who bestowed upon the rest of the world the main principles of their moral laws.

This third center of civilization is known by its ancient Babylonian name of Suri, or as we pronounce it, Syria.

The history of the people who lived in these

regions covers more than five thousand years.

It is a very, very complicated story.

I can not give you many details.

I shall try and weave their adventures into a single fabric, which will look like one of those marvelous rugs of which you read in the tales which Scheherazade told to Harun the Just.

五　象形文字的释明

在耶稣生前五十年，罗马人征服了沿地中海东岸诸地，在新得的领土之内，有一国叫作埃及。

在我们的历史中演了这样长一幕的罗马人，是讲实际的人类。

他们造桥，他们筑路，并且他们只用了不多，但是深有训练的军队和民政长官管领了大部的欧罗巴，东阿非利加和西亚细亚。

至于艺术和科学，他们并不感到深切的兴味。他们狐疑地以为能品箫或能写一首咏春之诗的人，是比较能走绳索的或教养得他的哈巴狗会用后足立起来的伶俐人稍高一筹而已。他们让那些事情给他们所藐视的希腊人和东方人去做，他们自己呢，只是日夜地整顿他们的本国和很多的领土所组成的大帝国。

当他们初到埃及时，埃及已古老得可惊了。

等到埃及人有历史时，早已过了六千五百余年。

在还没有人梦想到在台伯河的湿地中造一城市的好久之前，埃及的帝王们便已管领着广阔的领域，而以他们的宫殿为各种文化之中心了。

当罗马人还在野蛮，用笨拙的石斧狩猎狼和熊时，埃及人已在著书，已在施行微妙的医学上的手术，并已在教他们的小孩九九表了。

他们的发明中最重要而最惊奇的，要算他们的子子孙孙都能由此得益的，那保存他们口讲的语言和脑想的意思的艺术了。

我们称它做书写的艺术。

我们是这样地跟文字不可须臾离，竟不明白人们没有了书籍、报纸和杂志怎样能够生活着。

然而，他们是那样生活过了的。他们生存在这地球上的初期的百万年进步得如此之迟，这便是一个主要缘由。

他们是像猫狗般，只能教它们的小猫小狗一些简略的事情，如爬树见了生人便叫等类；因他们不能书写，他们便无法来袭用他们无数的祖先的经验了。

这唠叨得几乎可笑，不是吗？

为何对于如此平常的事情要这般的大惊小怪？

然而，当你写信时，你曾停过笔想过什么来没有？

比如你是到山中旅行而见了一只鹿。

你想将这个告诉给你住在城中的父亲听。

你怎么办？

你在一张纸上点了许多的点，划了许多的划，你更加了些点，划在信封上，并粘上了两分邮票，便将你的信投进邮政箱去了。

你真做了些什么来？

你将潦草的七弯八曲的字，代替了你口讲的言语。

然而你怎知你画了些这样的曲辫子，会使邮政局员和你的父亲重译做口讲的言语呢？

你知道，因为已经有人教过你画怎样的正确的形象便代替了怎样的口讲言语的声音。

我们稍用几个字母来看它们造成的法子。

我们发一喉音而写下了"G"。

我们让空气从我们紧闭着的牙齿流出而写下

了"S"。

我们张大了我们的嘴，如汽机般发出一音，那声音便是"H"。

这人类在几千百年中所发现的，给埃及人去成就了。

当然，他们并不是用印成这本书所用的字母。

他们有他们自己约组织。

那比我们所有的美丽得多，不过稍微复杂一些。

那是由房屋和农场四周的小物件的图像所组成的，如刀、犁、鸟、壶、盆等。他们的律法师将这些小图像刻画在庙宇的墙壁上，在他们死了的帝王的棺材上，和在干了的纸草的叶子上——我们"纸"的一字，就是从埃及的纸草一字而来。

但当罗马人进了这广大的藏书室时，他们显然地，既不消魂，又不动情。

他们有他们自己的文字的组织，他们以为它们要高超得多。

他们不知道希腊文（他们的字母是从这里学

得来的）是转从腓尼基文得来，而腓尼基文又是借助于古老的埃及文，才告完成的。他们不明白，他们也不留意。在他们的学校里面，只许教罗马文；所能满足了罗马小孩的，便能满足了任何人。

你会明白，在罗马长官的轻视和抵制之下，埃及的语言便不再存在了。这是已被忘却了。这种死去，正如我们有好几族的印第安人的语言已成为过去的事物一样。

继罗马人以管治埃及的阿拉伯人和土耳其人，憎恶一切与他们的圣经可兰（《古兰经》）所不同的文字。

后来在十六世纪的中叶，有几个西国的访游者来到埃及，而对于这些奇特的形象稍感兴味。

然而没有一个人解明它们的意义，而且，这些第一起来的欧罗巴人，只有跟那先他们来此的罗马人和土耳其人同等的智力。

事情发生了，在十八世纪的末叶，有一姓波那帕脱的法兰西将军来到了埃及。他并不是去研习古史。在军事上，他想用埃及来做他远征印度（不列颠的殖民地）的起点。这远征是完全失败了，然而他助成了解决古埃及文的神秘的问题。

在拿破仑波那帕脱的军队中，有一少年军官叫布鲁萨得的，他是屯扎尼罗河西口（这叫作罗塞达河）上的圣犹利安堡垒。

布鲁萨得喜欢在尼罗河下游的残墟中去详探细究；一日，他得到了一块石头，这使他十分地难以索解。

这像近处的别的东西一般，上面刻着象形文。

然而这块黑的火成石片跟以前所发现的都不同。

这上面刻着三种文字。快活啊！其中之一种是希腊文。

希腊文是懂得的。

这几乎可确定，那节埃及文包藏着希腊文的译文（或者说那节希腊文包藏着埃及文的译文），因此，启发古埃及文的钥匙，仿佛已发现了。

然而经过了三十余年艰深的研习，那适合那锁的钥匙方才制成。

于是神秘的门开了，而埃及的古代的宝藏室也只好献出它的秘密。

象形文字的探讨

那一生在阐解这种文字的工作的是冉弗朗沙善波力温——我们通常称他小善波力温以别于他的哥哥（他也是一个很博学的人）。

法兰西革命猝发时，小善波力温还是一个小孩，所以他避免了在波那帕脱将军的军队中服务。

当他的同胞接连地在得到荣耀的胜利时（也时常败下来，这是大军队所常有的事），善波力温在研究科普脱——埃及本国的基督教派——的语言。十九岁时，他被任命为一所小的法兰西大学的历史教授，在那里他开始他的翻译古埃及的象形文的伟大工作。

为此，他用了那块有名的罗塞达的黑石，就是那布鲁萨得在尼罗河口附近的残墟中所发现的。

那最初发现的石头依旧在埃及。拿破仑被逼得赶快地离去了这国度而顾不到那珍品了。后来英吉利人在一千八百零一年克复了亚历山大里亚，他们得到了那块石头，便带它到了伦敦去，便在今日你还可从英吉利博物院见到它。然而那刻文已抄了下来，带到了法兰西去，而给善波力温用去了。

希腊文是很清楚。刻着的是托勒密五世和他的妻子姑娄巴（就是莎士比亚所写的又一姑娄巴的祖母）的故事。然而其余的两种刻文还不曾献出它们的秘密。

其中之一种是象形文字，这是我们给有名的古埃及文的名字。这象形文字（Hieroglyphic）一字，是希腊文，意思是"圣刻"（Sacred carving）。这字用得很好，因它将这文体的目的和性质全给解明了。发明这种艺术的祭师不欲平民跟这深含神秘性的保藏着的语言太为接近。他们使文字成为一种圣的事业。

它满含着神秘和训令，因此象形文字的雕刻看做一种圣的艺术而不许人民为了如此平常的商业的目的而实习。

这条规例，在只有住在家里，而种植他们所需要的每种东西在自己田场内的纯朴的农民居住时，一径能通行着。但埃及渐成为一商埠，而那些经商的人，除了口讲的语言外，还需一种互达意思的方法。所以他们胆大地采用了祭师的小的图像，并为他们自己的利便，而将它们简单化了，自后他们用这一种新的文体写他们的商业信件，这便成了"民众的语言"，我们叫"民众的语言"也是根据了希腊文的原意而来的，

罗塞达石上的其余两种是希腊文的译文，一种是圣的，一种是民众的，而善波力温即由此二种文字从事他的研究。他尽力所能及地搜寻了各种埃及的文体，用来和罗塞达石比较而研究之，直到刻苦耐劳了二十年，才明白了十四个图像的意义。

那就是说，他每释明一个图像，要费去一年多的光阴。

后来他到埃及去，在一千八百二十三年他印出了他第一册以古象形文字为题的科学书，九年后他因操作过度而死了，他是个真实的殉于伟大的事业者，这事业在他童子时便已从事着。

然而，他人虽死，他的事业不死。

别人继续着他的工作。今日埃及古物学者能

读象形文字正如我们能读我们的新闻纸般容易。

二十年工夫只释明了十四个图像的工作似乎很慢。但是让我来告诉你们些善波力温的困难。于是你便会明白，你明白了，你便会叹服他的艰苦的工作。

古老的埃及人没用过简易的号语，他们越过了那一步。

自然，你是懂得号语是什么的。

每本印度的故事书里面都包含着一章异闻，那是用图像写的。小孩在某某种场合中，如猎牛者或印第安的战斗者，间有为他自己发明一种号语；一切的童子军全都懂得。然而埃及的很有些不同，我要用几个图像来给你解释清楚，比如你是善波力温在读一件古代的纸草片，那是讲到一住在尼罗河畔的农人。

忽然你读到一个持锯人的图像 。

“得啦，”你说，“那图像的意思，自然这农人出去锯下一株树来。你大概猜得不错。”

你又拿起一页象形文字。

里面是讲到一个年已八十二岁的皇后的故事。正在那页中间又看到了那同样的图像。至少，那是很踌躇了。皇后们是可以不用去锯树的。她们可以差别人代她们去做。年轻的皇后也许为操练的缘故而锯树，但八十二岁的皇后是跟她的猫儿和纺车住在屋内了。然而，那却有那图像。那画它的古时的祭师，既将它置在那儿，必定有一种意义。

他究竟有什么意义？

那谜语终究给善波力温解出了。

他发现埃及人是最早用我们所谓"谐音文字"的人。

正如其余许多含科学意思的字一样，"谐音"一字的语源是出于希腊。它的意思是"我们说话时所用的声音的科学"。你们早已见过这希腊字"phone"，这字的意思是声音。它出现于我们的"电话"（telephone）一词中，那是传递语声至远处的机器。

古时的埃及语是"谐音的"，这比号语的范围广得多。那原始式的号语，自穴居的人起始在他屋子的墙上刻画野兽的图像时，就已用着了。

现在让我们再回到那在讲老年皇后的故事中，突然出现的手拿锯子的小人儿处来一回。显然，他拿了锯子定有所做的。

"Saw"（锯子）或解作你可从木匠作中得到的一件器具，或解作动词"to see"（看）的既事式。

这是几世纪来这字所遇的遭际。

起初的意思是一人拿着一柄锯子。

继而这意思成了我们将三个现代字母 s，a 和 w 所拼缀着的发音。末了，将木匠器具的原意完全失去，而这图像便指了"看"的既事式。

这句仿古埃及的图像画成的现代英文句子会给你解明我的意思。

这或解作在你面部使你能看的两只圆东西，或解作"我"（I）（眼睛 eye 与 I 谐音。——译者注），就是在讲话或在写字的人。

这或指采蜜的，你想捉它时它会在你手指上刺一针的动物，或指动词"to be"，这字的发音相同而意思是"存在"（exist），这字还可做动词如"be-come"（变成），"be-have"（行为）

的前半字。同样蜜蜂（bee）的下面接着的 我们推知是指"leave"（生叶子）或"leaf"（叶子）一字的发音的。将你的"bee"和"leaf"放在一起，那你便得到了缀成这动词"bee-leave"或照如今我们所写的"believe"（相信）的二个字音。

"眼睛"，你是已知道了。

末了的一个图像 好像是只长颈鹿。这是只长颈鹿，并且这还是古号语的一部分，凡那觉得甚是利便的，便被继续着采用。

于是，你得到下面的一个句子，"我相信我看见了一只长颈鹿"（I believe I saw a giraffe）。

这种组织，一经发明，便被几千年来地改进着。

渐渐地许多最重要的图像变成了简易的字母或简短的字音如"fu""em""dee"或"zee"，或如我们所写的 f，m，d 和 z。有了这些字的帮助，埃及人能写下任何他们所想写下的题材，并能毫不困难地将这一代的经验保存了，以便利于后代的子孙。

一句话，那就是善波力温用了他过度的，以

至在他少年时即被戕杀了的过度的研求所教给我们的。

　　那也就是我们今日知道埃及的历史较任何别一个古国都清楚一些的理由。

V. THE KEY OF STONE

FIFTY years before the birth of Christ, the Romans conquered the land along the eastern shores of the Mediterranean and among this newly acquired territory was a country called Egypt.

The Romans, who are to play such a great role in our history, were a race of practical men.

They built bridges, they constructed roads, and with a small but highly trained army of soldiers and civil officers, they managed to rule the greater part of Europe, of eastern Africa and western Asia.

As for art and the sciences, these did not interest them very much. They regarded with suspicion a man who could play the lute or who could write a poem about Spring and only thought him little better than the clever fellow who could walk the tightrope or who had trained his poodle dog to stand on its hind legs. They left such things to the Greeks and to the Orientals, both of whom they despised, while they themselves spent their days and nights keeping order among the thousand and one nations of their vast empire.

When they first set foot in Egypt that country was already terribly old.

More than six thousand and five hundred years had gone by since the history of the Egyptian people had begun.

Long before any one had dreamed of building a city amidst the swamps of the river Tiber, the kings of Egypt had ruled far and wide and had made their court the center of all civilization.

While the Romans were still savages who chased wolves and bears with clumsy stone axes, the Egyptians were writing books, performing intricate medical operations and teaching their children the tables of multiplication.

This great progress they owed chiefly to one very wonderful invention, to the art of preserving their spoken words and their ideas for the benefit of their children and grandchildren.

We call this the art of writing.

We are so familiar with writing that we can not understand how people ever managed to live without books and newspapers and magazines.

But they did and it was the main reason why they made such slow progress during the first million years of their stay upon this planet.

They were like cats and dogs who can only teach their puppies and their kittens a few simple things (barking at a stranger and climbing trees and such things) and who, because they can not write, possess no way in which they can use the experience of their countless ancestors.

This sounds almost funny, doesn't it?

And why make such a fuss about so simple a matter?

But did you ever stop to think what happens when you write a letter?

Suppose that you are taking a trip in the

mountains and you have seen a deer.

You want to tell this to your father who is in the city.

What do you do?

You put a lot of dots and dashes upon a piece of paper—you add a few more dots and dashes upon an envelope and you carry your epistle to the mailbox together with a two-cent stamp.

What have you really been doing?

You have changed a number of spoken words into a number of pothooks and scrawls.

But how did you know how to make your curlycues in such a fashion that both the postman and your father could retranslate them into spoken words?

You knew, because some one had taught you how to draw the precise figures which represented the sound of your spoken words.

Just take a few letters and see the way this game is played.

We make a guttural noise and write down a "G".

We let the air pass through our closed teeth and we write down "S".

We open our mouth wide and make a noise like a steam engine and the sound is written down "H".

It took the human race hundreds of thousands of years to discover this and the credit for it goes to the Egyptians.

Of course they did not use the letters which have been used to print this book.

They had a system of their own.

It was much prettier than ours but not quite so simple.

It consisted of little figures and images of things around the house and around the farm, of knives and plows and birds and pots and pans. These little figures their scribes scratched and painted upon the wall of the temples, upon the coffins of their dead kings and upon the dried leaves of the papyrus plant which has given its name to our "paper".

But when the Romans entered this vast library they showed neither enthusiasm nor interest.

They possessed a system of writing of their own which they thought vastly superior.

They did not know that the Greeks (from whom they had learned their alphabet) had in turn obtained theirs from the Phoenicians who had again borrowed with great success from the old Egyptians. They did not know and they did not care. In their schools the Roman alphabet was taught exclusively and what was good enough for the Roman children was good enough for everybody else.

You will understand that the Egyptian language did not long survive the indifference and the opposition of the Roman governors. It was forgotten. It died just as the languages of most of our Indian tribes have become a thing of the past.

The Arabs and the Turks who succeeded the Romans as the rulers of Egypt abhorred all writing that was not connected with their holy book, the Koran.

At last in the middle of the sixteenth century a few western visitors came to Egypt and showed a mild interest in these strange pictures.

But there was no one to explain their meaning and these first Europeans were as wise as the Romans and the Turks had been before them.

Now it happened, late in the eighteenth century that a certain French general by the name of Buonaparte visited Egypt. He did not go there to study ancient history. He wanted to use the country as a starting point for a military expedition against the British colonies in India. This expedition failed completely but it helped solve the mysterious problem of the ancient Egyptian writing.

Among the soldiers of Napoleon Buonaparte there was a young officer by the name of Broussard. He was stationed at the fortress of St. Julien on the western mouth of the Nile which is called the Rosetta river.

Broussard liked to rummage among the ruins of the lower Nile and one day he found a stone which greatly puzzled him.

Like everything else in that neighborhood, it was

covered with picture writing.

But this slab of black basalt was different from anything that had ever been discovered.

It carried three inscriptions and one of these (oh joy!) was in Greek.

The Greek language was known.

As it was almost certain that the Egyptian part contained a translation of the Greek (or vice versa), the key to ancient Egyptian seemed to have been discovered.

But it took more than thirty years of very hard work before the key had been made to fit the lock.

Then the mysterious door was opened and the ancient treasure house of Egypt was forced to surrender its secrets.

The man who gave his life to the task of deciphering this language was Jean Francois Champollion—usually called Champollion Junior to distinguish him from his older brother who was also a very learned man.

Champollion Junior was a baby when the French

revolution broke out and therefore he escaped serving in the armies of the General Buonaparte.

While his countrymen were marching from one glorious victory to another (and back again as such Imperial armies are apt to do) Champollion studied the language of the Copts, the native Christians of Egypt. At the age of nineteen he was appointed a professor of History at one of the smaller French universities and there he began his great work of translating the pictures of the old Egyptian language.

For this purpose he used the famous black stone of Rosetta which Broussard had discovered among the ruins near the mouth of the Nile.

The original stone was still in Egypt. Napoleon had been forced to vacate the country in a hurry and he had left this curiosity behind. When the English retook Alexandria in the year 1801 they found the stone and carried it to London, where you may see it this very day in the British Museum. The Inscriptions however had been copied and had been taken to France, where they were used by Champollion.

The Greek text was quite clear. It contained the story of Ptolemy V and his wife Cleopatra, the grandmother of that other Cleopatra about whom Shakespeare wrote. The other two inscriptions, however, refused to surrender their secrets.

One of them was in hieroglyphics, the name we give to the oldest known Egyptian writing. The word *hieroglyphic* is Greek and means "sacred carving". It is a very good name for it fully describes the purpose and nature of this script. The priests who had invented this art did not want the common people to become too familiar with the deep mysteries of preserving speech. They made writing a sacred business.

They surrounded it with much mystery and decreed that the carving of hieroglyphics be regarded as a sacred art and forbade the people to practice it for such a common purpose as business or commerce.

They could enforce this rule with success so long as the country was inhabited by simple farmers who lived at home and grew everything they needed upon their own fields. But gradually Egypt became a land of traders and these traders needed a means of communication beyond the spoken word. So they boldly took the little figures of the priests and simplified them for their own purposes. Thereafter they wrote their business letters in the new script which became known as the "popular language" and which we call by its Greek name, the "Demotic language".

The Rosetta stone carried both the sacred and the popular translations of the Greek text and upon these two Champollion centered his attack. He collected every piece of Egyptian script which he could get and together with the Rosetta stone he compared and studied them until after twenty years of patient drudgery he understood the meaning of fourteen little figures.

That means that he spent more than a whole year to decipher each single picture.

Finally he went to Egypt and in the year 1823 he

printed the first scientific book upon the subject of the ancient hieroglyphics.

Nine years later he died from overwork, as a true martyr to the great task which he had set himself as a boy.

His work, however, lived after him.

Others continued his studies and today Egyptologists can read hieroglyphics as easily as we can read the printed pages of our newspapers.

Fourteen pictures in twenty years seems very slow work. But let me tell you something of Champollion's difficulties. Then you will understand, and understanding, you will admire his courage.

The old Egyptians did not use a simple sign language. They had passed beyond that stage.

Of course, you know what sign language is.

Every Indian story has a chapter about queer messages, written in the form of little pictures. Hardly a boy but at some stage or other of his life, as a buffalo hunter or an Indian fighter, has invented a sign language of his own, and all Boy Scouts are familiar with it. But Egyptian was something quite different and I must try and make this clear to you with a few pictures. Suppose that you were Champollion and that you were reading an old papyrus which told the story of a farmer who lived somewhere along the banks of the river Nile.

Suddenly you came across a picture of a man with a saw .

"Very well," you said, "that means, of course, that the farmer went out and cut a tree down." Most likely you had guessed correctly.

Next you took another page of hieroglyphics.

They told the story of a queen who had lived to be eighty-two years old. Right in the middle of the text the same picture occurred. That was very puzzling, to say the least. Queens do not go about cutting down trees. They let other people do it for them. A young queen may saw wood for the sake of exercise, but a queen of eighty-two stays at home with her cat and her spinning wheel. Yet, the picture was there. The ancient priest who drew it must have placed it there for a definite purpose.

What could he have meant?

That was the riddle which Champollion finally solved.

He discovered that the Egyptians were the first people to use what we call "phonetic writing".

Like most other words which express a scientific idea, the word "phonetic" is of Greek origin. It means the "science of the sound which is made by our speech". You have seen the Greek word "phone", which means the voice, before. It occurs in our word "telephone", the machine which carries the voice to a distant point.

Ancient Egyptian was "phonetic" and it set man free from the narrow limits of that sign language which in some primitive form had been used ever since the cave-dweller began to scratch pictures of wild animals upon the walls of his home.

Now let us return for a moment to the little fellow with his saw who suddenly appeared in the story of the old queen. Evidently he had something to do with a saw.

A "saw" is either a tool which you find in a carpenter shop or it means the past tense of the verb "to see".

This is what had happened to the word during the course of many centuries.

First of all it had meant a man with a saw.

Then it came to mean the sound which we reproduce by the three modern letters, s, a and w. In the end the original meaning of carpentering was lost entirely and the picture indicated the past tense of "to see".

A modern English sentence done into the images of ancient Egypt will show you what I mean.

The ⌞•⌟ means either these two round objects in your head which allow you to see, or it means "I", the person who is talking or writing.

A 🐝 is either an animal which gathers honey

and pricks you in the finger when you try to catch it, or it represents to verb "to be", which is pronounced the same way and which means to "exist". Again it may be the first part of a verb like "be-come" or "be-have". In this case the bee is followed by a ⬥ which represents the sound which we find in the word "leave" or "leaf". Put your "bee" and your "leaf" together and you have the two sounds which make the verb "bee-leave" or "believe" as we write it nowadays.

The "eye" you know all about.

Finally you get a picture which looks like a giraffe. 🦒 It is a giraffe, and it is part of the old sign language, which has been continued wherever it seemed most convenient.

Therefore you get the following sentence, "I believe I saw a giraffe."

This system, once invented, was developed during thousands of years.

Gradually the most important figures came to mean single letters or short sounds like "fu" or "em" or "dee" or "zee", or as we write them, f and m and d and z. And with the help of these, the Egyptians could write anything they wanted upon every conceivable subject, and could preserve the experience of one generation for the benefit of the next without the slightest difficulty.

That, in a very general way, is what Champollion taught us after the exhausting search which killed him when he was a young man.

That too, is the reason why today we know Egyptian history better than that of any other ancient country.

六　生之区与死之域

人的历史是一饥饿的生物寻求食物的记录。

那里食物多而容易得到的，人便到那里去建他的家。

尼罗河流域的声名一定在很早的日子便远播着了。从各处来的野民群居在尼罗河的两岸。尼罗河的四周全被沙漠和海包围着，所以除了坚毅卓越的男子和女子外，到这肥沃的牧场来的甚是不易。

我们不知道他们是谁。有的来自阿非利加的中部，他们有卷曲的头发和厚的嘴唇。

有的皮肤略带黄色的从阿拉伯的沙漠和西亚细亚的宽广之河的那面来。

他们彼此为要占此奇境而战争。

他们造好了的村庄被他们的邻人毁坏，于是他们也去从那反被他们克服了的别一邻人处，夺取砖瓦来重造他们的村庄。

　　后来有一新的种族发达起来了。他们自称
"来密"，这不过是"人们"的意思。他们对这名
字很觉自豪，而且他们用这个名称犹之我们说美
利坚是"上帝自己的国家"一样的意思。

　　当尼罗河的年潮泛滥的时季，他们居住在一
个乡村中的小岛上，这个小岛为了有海和沙漠，
是跟世界的别部隔离着的。无疑地，这些人民是
我们所称的"独幅的"，他们有乡居者的习惯，
很少跟他们的邻人们有所接触。

　　他们是唯我独尊的。他们想他们的风俗，习
惯终要比任何别族的都要好些。同样，他们以为
他们自己的神祇要比别国的神祇有力。他们并非
真是轻视外国人，不过对他们似有些可怜；如可
能，他们不让他们住在埃及的领土内，恐怕他们
本族的人民会给"洋气"所同化。

　　他们是善心的，很少做残忍的事。他们是有
耐性的，在事业之中他们是无所争的。生命是一
平淡的赋予，他们把它看得很随便，从不像北方
的居民般只为生存而竞争。

　　当太阳从血红的沙漠尽头的地平线升起时，
他们到田间去工作。当太阳的最后的光线从山

边隐下去时，他们回去
睡觉。

　　他们刻苦地工作，
跋涉，并用他们无智的
淡漠和绝对的忍耐以
忍受那所发生的无论什
么事。

死之域

　　他们相信这生命不
过是那新的存在的引端，那新的存在当死亡驾临
时才开始，直到后来，埃及人看未来的生命远重
于现世的生命时，他们便从繁殖的田地而转入于
一洪大的神殿里去供奉死人。

　　因为大都的古流域的纸草卷讲的是宗教事情
的故事，我们很准确地知道埃及人敬畏些什么神
和他们怎样尽力于为那些已进永息之乡的人们谋
种种的幸福和安适。起初每一小村各自有一神。

　　这神常被假定居在奇形的石头里面，或特大
的树枝里面。跟他做好朋友是有益的，因他能
降灾，并能毁坏收获和延长天旱的时期，直至
人民和牛羊全被干死了为止。所以村民赠与他
礼物——有时供奉东西给他吃，有时供奉一束

鲜花。

当埃及人去和仇敌开战时。神祇是一定与俱的，甚至当他为一面战旗，在危急时，人民便在他的四周嘲笑他。

但当立国渐久，较好的街道也已筑好，埃及人也开始出外游行去了之后，那旧日的"非的希"（fetishes——神祇，就是这种木石块的称呼）便失去了他们重要的意义，而被毁灭了，或被弃在不注意的墙角边，或用来做阶石或椅子。

他们的地位是被那些较前者更有力的新的神祇占据去，他们是些影响着全流域的埃及人生命的自然力。

其中第一位神是使万物生长的太阳。

次之是尼罗河，这节制着日中的热度，并从河底带上丰富的黏土以使田地润泽而肥沃。

再次是在晚上乘着她的小舟划过弓似的天空的柔和的月；还有雷、电和任何种能祸福于生命的东西——依照他们的喜悦和嗜好。

现在我们可以在屋上植避雷针，或是造蓄水池以备夏季无雨时，不至绝了我们的生命。但是完全听命于自然之力的古人，却不容易处置它们。

反之，它们成了在他的日常生活中所弃不了的一部——自他刚放进摇篮直到他的身体预备作永息的那日止，它们老伴着他。

他毫不能意想到此种广大而有力的现象，如电光之闪烁或江河之泛滥，只是非具人性的事物。或人——或物——得做它们的主人，而管理它们，如机师之处治他的机器，或船主之驾驶他的船只。

于是总神被创立了，如军队之有主帅。

在他的治下有班低级的属员。

在他们自己的领地以内，各自能独立行动。

然而，在影响全民众幸福的重要事情上，他们得服从他们上司的命令。

埃及的无上神圣的主宰是叫作奥赛烈司。他的一生神奇的故事，一切的埃及的小孩全知道。

从前在尼罗河流域，有过一个名叫奥赛烈司的王。

他是一个善人；他教给他的百姓怎样耕种他们的田地；他为他的国度定了公正的律法。但是，他有一个恶的兄弟，他的名字叫塞司。

现在，为了他是如此的善良，塞司嫉妒奥赛烈司。一日，他请奥赛烈司去赴宴；后来他说，他愿意给他看些东西。好奇的奥赛烈司问这是什么；塞司说这是式样滑稽的棺材，这会使人像穿套衣服般的合适。奥赛烈司说他愿意试试。所以他卧进了这棺材，但是他刚进去便"嘭"的一声——塞司盖了盖。于是塞司召集了他的仆人，并命令他们将这棺材掷进尼罗河中去。

不久他的可怕的作为的信息传遍了全地。埃西，深爱她丈夫的奥赛烈司的妻子，立刻到尼罗河畔去；不多一会儿波浪将棺材冲上了岸来。于是她前去告诉她的儿子和刺斯，他在另一地方管理着。但是她刚刚离开，这可恶的兄弟塞司便打进了皇宫而将奥赛烈司的身体割做十四块。

埃西回来时，她觉察了塞司所做的事。她便拿起了十四块死尸而将它们缝合。于是奥赛烈司复活了。他便永远永远地做着管理第二世界的王，这人们的已离了身体的灵魂都一定要经过的。

至于塞司，恶者，他想逃避，但是奥赛烈司和埃西的儿子和刺斯早顺了他母亲的警告，捉了他并杀了他。

　　这有一忠心的妻子，一可恶的兄弟和一尽职的儿子（他为他父亲复了仇的），而且这最后的胜利是善胜服了恶的故事，成了埃及人的宗教命脉的基础。

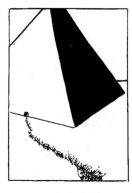

金字塔

　　奥赛烈司是奉为全生物，就是那在冬日似乎死去，然而到了次春仍能复苏的生物之神。因是来生的主宰，他末了审讯人们的行为，并且致祸于曾用残忍，奸诈和虐待过弱者的人。

　　至于死人灵魂的世界，是在西方之高山的那面（这也就是年幼的尼罗之家）。埃及人要说有人已死了时，便说他"已归了西"。

　　埃西跟她的丈夫奥赛烈司同享着崇奉和敬意。被奉为太阳神的他们的儿子和刺斯——太阳从那里落下去的"地平线"之一字即从此而来——成了新系的埃及王之第一位，并且一切的埃及的法老全将和刺斯做了他们的中名。

　　自然，每一小城小村还继续着崇拜少数的他

们自己的神祇。但是就大体而言，一切的人民都承认奥赛烈司的最高权能而欲得到他的恩赐。

这不是件不足重轻的事情，而且引出了许多的奇俗。第一件，埃及人相信，如其不能保存那曾寄住于这世界过的身体，灵魂便不得进奥赛烈司之王国。

无论怎样，死后的身体终得保存，且得给它一永久而安适的家。所以人一经死后，他的尸首便立刻以香料保存之。这是种艰难而复杂的手术。这种手术是由一半医生半教士的官员同一副手（他的职司是在胸部开一从此放进柏油，末药和肉桂的裂缝）的助力完成的。这副手是属于所视为人们中最被轻蔑的特种人民。埃及人想肯做这种施暴力于人（无论活的或死的）的事情是可惊的；只有下等之最下等者才能被雇来做这种背民心的工作。

自后，教士重取了那身体，放进一种天然碳酸钠（这是专为此用从

金字塔的筑成

辽远的利比亚沙漠取来的）的溶液中，浸十星期之久。于是这身体已经成为"干尸"，因为这是满充以"末米亚"或柏油。这是裹裹重裹裹地裹在一种特备的麻布里面，而将它放进一美丽地装饰了的木棺材，以备给运到它的西方沙漠的最后之家。

坟墓是一小间在沙漠的沙土之中的石屋，或者是在山边的一个空洞。

棺材已在中央放好后，这间小屋便布置以厨房器具，兵器和形似面包师和屠夫的偶像（泥的或木的），他们是指望侍候他们的死了的主人的，如其他有所需要时。更加上了笛和提琴，以给这坟墓之占据者消遣他在这"永远之家"中所必须度过的长时间。

于是屋顶被沙覆盖着，而这死埃及人是静止于这长眠的安息中。

然而沙漠中是满布了狼和鬣狗等野兽；它们掘穿了木屋顶和沙土而进去吃了那干尸。

这是最可怕的，因为自后这灵魂是命定着永远的漂泊，遭受着人之无家般的烦闷。求这尸首的万全计，坟墓之四周筑着一道矮的砖墙；中空

干尸

的地方实以泥沙和细石。这样做了，便造成了一座人工的低的小山，因此这干尸可免了野兽和劫夺者的侵袭。

一日有一埃及人刚安葬好了他所曾特殊爱好的母亲，他便决定给她一种要超越一切在尼罗河流域中所曾经建筑过的纪念品。

他召集了他的农奴，叫他们造一几哩路外便能看见的人工的山。在这山的上面他盖一层砖瓦，使那泥沙不至被吹去。

人民喜欢这意思的新奇。

马上他们各不相让地设法超前，坟墓便离地面二十呎（英尺旧也作呎），三十呎，四十呎地高起来了。

末了，一有钱的贵族，定造一筑以坚石的殡舍。

在安放干尸的真正的坟墓的顶上，他筑着高入空中几百呎的砖瓦垒。有一小小的过道通进地罗；当这过道用一块重大的花岗石板闭住后，干尸避免了一切的闯入而得安全。

自然，王在这种事情中不能给他的百姓胜过。他是全埃及最有势力的人。他是住在最大的房屋中，所以他是应得最好的坟墓。

别人所用砖瓦做的，他能用更贵重的材料做。

法老差遣他的官员到各处去召集工人。他筑路。他造营房给工人住和睡（即在今日你还可看见那些营房）。于是他动工，给他自己建一永远不灭的坟墓。

我们叫这一大堆的石工做"金字塔"。

这字的来源是奇异的。

当希腊人游访埃及时，金字塔已经有了几千年了。

自然，埃及人招待他们的来客去沙漠中看这些奇观，正如我们招待外国人去察视武尔威士塔和布鲁克林桥一般。

叹服之至的希腊客人挥他的手，问这奇异的山是什么。

他的向导想他在问这非常的高度，便说"是

的，它们真是很高"。

埃及的高字是"piremus"。

希腊人一定想这是全建筑的名字，给了它一希腊文的语尾，他叫它做"pyramis"。

我们已将 s 换了 d，然而我们仍用的一样的埃及字，当我们谈及沿尼罗河畔之石墓。

这许多金字塔中最大的（它是造在五十世纪以前），是五百呎高。

在墙脚它是七百五十五呎宽。

它占了十三余亩的沙漠地，这是等于圣彼得礼拜堂——基督教世界之最大的建筑——所占的地面三倍那么多。

在二十年中，十万以上的人用来从辽远的西奈半岛运石头——渡它们过尼罗河（他们怎样处理这事，我们不明白）——适中地拖它们过沙漠；终究扯起它们于适合的位置中。

然而法老的建筑师和工程师完成他们的工作如此的尽善，以至于就是通进金字塔中皇陵的窄狭的过道，虽然从各方面压下来千千万万吨石头的可惊的重量，都不会被压得变了样。

VI. THE LAND OF THE LIVING AND THE LAND OF THE DEAD

THE history of Man is the record of a hungry creature in search of food.

Wherever food was plentiful and easily gathered, thither man travelled to make his home.

The fame of the Nile valley must have spread at an early date. From far and wide, wild people flocked to the banks of the river. Surrounded on all sides by desert or sea, it was not easy to reach these fertile fields and only the hardiest men and women survived.

We do not know who they were. Some came from the interior of Africa and had woolly hair and thick lips.

Others, with a yellowish skin, came from the desert of Arabia and the broad rivers of western Asia.

They fought each other for the possession of this wonderful land.

They built villages which their neighbors destroyed and they rebuilt them with the bricks they had taken from other neighbors whom they in turn had vanquished.

Gradually a new race developed. They called themselves "remi", which means simply "the Men". There was a touch of pride in this name and they used it in the same sense that we refer to America as "God's own country".

Part of the year, during the annual flood of the Nile, they lived on small islands within a country which itself was cut off from the rest of the world by the sea and the desert. No wonder that these people were what we call "insular", and had the habits of villagers who rarely come in contact with their neighbors.

They liked their own ways best. They thought their own habits and customs just a trifle better than those of anybody else. In the same way, their own gods were considered more powerful than the gods of other nations. They did not exactly despise foreigners, but they felt a mild pity for them and if possible they kept them outside of the Egyptian domains, lest their own people be corrupted by "foreign notions".

They were kind-hearted and rarely did anything that was cruel. They were patient and in business dealings they were rather indifferent. Life came as an easy gift and they never became stingy and mean like northern people who have to struggle for mere existence.

When the sun arose above the blood-red horizon of the distant desert, they went forth to till their fields. When the last rays of light had disappeared beyond the mountain ridges, they went to bed.

They worked hard, they plodded and they bore whatever happened with stolid unconcern and profound patience.

They believed that this life was but a short preface to a new existence which began the moment

Death had entered the house. Until at last, the life of the future came to be regarded as more important than the life of the present and the people of Egypt turned their teeming land into one vast shrine for the worship of the dead.

And as most of the papyrus-rolls of the ancient valley tell stories of a religious nature we know with great accuracy just what gods the Egyptians revered and how they tried to assure all possible happiness and comfort to those who had entered upon the eternal sleep. In the beginning each little village had possessed a god of its own.

Often this god was supposed to reside in a queerly shaped stone or in the branch of a particularly large tree. It was well to be good friends with him for he could do great harm and destroy the harvest and prolong the period of drought until the people and the cattle had all died of thirst. Therefore the villages made him presents—offered him things to eat or a bunch of flowers.

When the Egyptians went forth to fight their

enemies the god must be taken along, until he became a sort of battle flag around which the people rallied in time of danger.

But when the country grew older and better roads had been built and the Egyptians had begun to travel, the old "fetishes", as such chunks of stone and wood were called, lost their importance and were thrown away or were left in a neglected corner or were used as doorsteps or chairs.

Their place was taken by new gods who were more powerful than the old ones had been and who represented those forces of nature which influenced the lives of the Egyptians of the entire valley.

First among these was the Sun which makes all things grow.

Next came the river Nile which tempered the heat of the day and brought rich deposits of clay to refresh the fields and make them fertile.

Then there was the kindly Moon which at night rowed her little boat across the arch of heaven and there was Thunder and there was Lightning and there were any number of things which could make life happy or miserable according to their pleasure and desire.

Ancient man, entirely at the mercy of these forces of nature, could not get rid of them as easily as we do when we plant lightning rods upon our houses or build reservoirs which keep us alive during the summer months when there is no rain.

On the contrary they formed an intimate part of his daily life—they accompanied him from the moment he was put into his cradle until the day that his body was prepared for eternal rest.

Neither could he imagine that such vast and powerful phenomena as a bolt of lightning or the flood of a river were mere impersonal things. Some one—somewhere—must be their master and must direct them as the engineer directs his engine or a captain steers his ship.

A God-in-Chief was therefore created, like the commanding general of an army.

A number of lower officers were placed at his

disposal.

Within their own territory each one could act independently.

In grave matters, however, which affected the happiness of all the people, they must take orders from their master.

The Supreme Divine Ruler of the land of Egypt was called Osiris, and all the little Egyptian children knew the story of his wonderful life.

Once upon a time, in the valley of the Nile, there lived a king called Osiris.

He was a good man who taught his subjects how to till their fields and who gave his country just laws. But he had a bad brother whose name was Seth.

Now Seth envied Osiris because he was so virtuous and one day he invited him to dinner and afterwards he said that he would like to show him something. Curious Osiris asked what it was and Seth said that it was a funnily shaped coffin which fitted one like a suit of clothes. Osiris said that he would like to try it. So he lay down in the coffin but no sooner was he inside when bang!—Seth shut the lid. Then he called for his servants and ordered them to throw the coffin into the Nile.

Soon the news of his terrible deed spread throughout the land. Isis, the wife of Osiris, who had loved her husband very dearly, went at once to the banks of the Nile, and after a short while the waves threw the coffin upon the shore. Then she went forth to tell her son Horus, who ruled in another land, but no sooner had she left than Seth, the wicked brother, broke into the palace and cut the body of Osiris into fourteen pieces.

When Isis returned, she discovered what Seth had done. She took the fourteen pieces of the dead body and sewed them together and then Osiris came back to life and reigned for ever and ever as king of the lower world to which the souls of men must travel after they have left the body.

As for Seth, the Evil One, he tried to escape, but Horus, the son of Osiris and Isis, who had been warned by his mother, caught him and slew him.

This story of a faithful wife and a wicked brother and a dutiful son who avenged his father and the final victory of virtue over wickedness formed the basis of the religious life of the people of Egypt.

Osiris was regarded as the god of all living things which seemingly die in the winter and yet return to renewed existence the next spring. As ruler of the Life Hereafter, he was the final judge of the acts of men, and woe unto him who had been cruel and unjust and had oppressed the weak.

As for the world of the departed souls, it was situated beyond the high mountains of the west (which was also the home of the young Nile) and when an Egyptian wanted to say that someone had died, he said that he "had gone west".

Isis shared the honors and the duties of Osiris with him. Their son Horus, who was worshipped as the god of the Sun (hence the word "horizon", the place where the sun sets) became the first of a new line of Egyptian kings and all the Pharaohs of Egypt had Horus as their middle name.

Of course, each little city and every small village continued to worship a few divinities of their own. But generally speaking, all the people recognized the sublime power of Osiris and tried to gain his favor.

This was no easy task, and led to many strange customs. In the first place, the Egyptians came to believe that no soul could enter into the realm of Osiris without the possession of the body which had been its place of residence in this world.

Whatever happened, the body must be preserved after death, and it must be given a permanent and suitable home. Therefore as soon as a man had died, his corpse was embalmed. This was a difficult and complicated operation which was performed by an official who was half doctor and half priest, with the help of an assistant whose duty was to make the incision through which the chest could be filled with cedar-tree pitch and myrrh and cassia. This assistant belonged to a special class of people who were counted among the most despised of men. The Egyptians thought it a terrible thing to commit acts of violence upon a human being, whether dead or living, and only the lowest of the low could be hired to perform this unpopular task.

Afterwards the priest took the body again and for a period of ten weeks he allowed it to be soaked in a solution of natron which was brought for this purpose from the distant desert of Libya. Then the body had become a "mummy" because it was filled with "Mumiai" or pitch. It was wrapped in yards and yards of specially prepared linen and it was placed in a beautifully decorated wooden coffin, ready to be removed to its final home in the western desert.

The grave itself was a little stone room in the sand of the desert or a cave in a hill-side.

After the coffin had been placed in the center the little room was well supplied with cooking utensils and weapons and statues (of clay or wood) representing bakers and butchers who were expected to wait upon their dead master in case he needed anything. Flutes and fiddles were added to give the occupant of the grave a chance to while away the long hours which he must spend in this "house of eternity".

Then the roof was covered with sand and the dead Egyptian was left to the peaceful rest of eternal sleep.

But the desert is full of wild creatures, hyenas and wolves, and they dug their way through the wooden roof and the sand and ate up the mummy.

This was a terrible thing, for then the soul was doomed to wander forever and suffer agonies of a man without a home. To assure the corpse all possible safety a low wall of brick was built around the grave and the open space was filled with sand and gravel. In this way a low artificial hill was made which protected the mummy against wild animals and robbers.

Then one day, an Egyptian who had just buried his Mother, of whom he had been particularly fond, decided to give her a monument that should surpass anything that had ever been built in the valley of the Nile.

He gathered his serfs and made them build an artificial mountain that could be seen for miles around. The sides of this hill he covered with a layer of bricks that the sand might not be blown away.

People liked the novelty of the idea.

Soon they were trying to outdo each other and the graves rose twenty and thirty and forty feet above the ground.

At last a rich nobleman ordered a burial chamber made of solid stone.

On top of the actual grave where the mummy rested, he constructed a pile of bricks which rose several hundred feet into the air. A small passage-way gave entrance to the vault and when this passage was closed with a heavy slab of granite the mummy was safe from all intrusion.

The King of course could not allow one of his subjects to outdo him in such a matter. He was the most powerful man of all Egypt who lived in the biggest house and therefore he was entitled to the best grave.

What others had done in brick he could do with the help of more costly materials.

Pharaoh sent his officers far and wide to gather workmen. He constructed roads. He built barracks in which the workmen could live and sleep (you may see those barracks this very day). Then he set to work and made himself a grave which was to endure for all time.

We call this great pile of masonry a "pyramid".

The origin of the word is a curious one.

When the Greeks visited Egypt the Pyramids were already several thousand years old.

Of course the Egyptians took their guests into the desert to see these wondrous sights just as we take foreigners to gaze at the Wool-worth Tower and Brooklyn Bridge.

The Greek guest, lost in admiration, waved his hands and asked what the strange mountains might be.

His guide thought that he referred to the extraordinary height and said, "Yes, they are very high indeed."

The Egyptian word for height was "piremus."

The Greek must have thought that this was the name of the whole structure and giving it a Greek ending he called it a "pyramis".

We have changed the "s" into a "d" but we still use the same Egyptian word when we talk of the stone graves along the banks of the Nile.

The biggest of these many pyramids, which was built fifty centuries ago, was five hundred feet high.

At the base it was seven hundred and fifty-five feet wide.

It covered more than thirteen acres of desert, which is three times as much space as that occupied by the church of Saint Peter, the largest edifice of the Christian world.

During twenty years, over a hundred thousand men were used to carry the stones from the distant peninsula of Sinai—to ferry them across the Nile (how they ever managed to do this we do not understand)—to drag them halfway across the desert and finally hoist them into their correct position.

But so well did Pharaoh's architects and engineers perform their task that the narrow passage-way which leads to the royal tomb in the heart of the pyramid has never yet been pushed out of shape by the terrific weight of those thousands and thousands of tons of stone which press upon it from all sides.

七　国家之建立

如今我们全是"国家"的一分子。

我们也许是法兰西人或者中国人或者俄罗斯人；我们也许住在印度尼希亚（你们知道那是在哪儿）的最远之一角，然而，无论怎样，我们都属于那新奇的人民的组织，这叫作"国家"。

这没有什么关系，无论我们承认王，皇帝或总统做我们的元首。我们生死全是这大团体之一小分子，而且没一人能逃避了这命运。

其实"国家"实在是一个新近的发明。

世界的最初的居民并不知道它是什么。

每一家族，生，打猎，工作和死都只为自己而且孤立。有时也有为了扩大抵抗野兽和别族野民之力起见，少数的家族联合成一宽弛的同盟，这叫作部落。但是一经危险已过，这几群人民便立刻仍各自为己，各自孤立。如其这弱者不能保护他们自己的洞穴，他们便只好听命于鬣狗和老虎，而且没有一个人深为悲伤，如其他们是被杀了。

简而言之，每人对他自己一种族；于邻居的幸福和安全他不负责任。这是渐渐地渐渐地改变了。埃及是第一个国度，在那里人民组织成了一个整理完美的帝国。

尼罗河对这有用的进化是负了直接的责任的。我已经对你们说过，在每年的夏季，大部的尼罗流域和尼罗之三角砂洲怎样地变成了广漠的陆地上之海。从这水得到了最大的利益，然而泛滥也是致命之患，这时必须在某种地方造坝和小岛，这会供给人和走兽一避难地，当八九两月时，虽然这些小的人工岛的建造是并非简易的。

没有别人帮助，单单一人或单单一家族或甚至一个小的部落，不能建造河坝。

每当河中的水开始上涨，使农人和他的妻子儿女以及家畜感到毁灭的恐惧，即使他不喜欢邻居，为了怕溺死的缘故，也不得不去访问全村落的人。

“需要”逼得人民忘了他们的微小的差异，不久全尼罗河流域都给人民的小结合占据着。他

们常为共同的目的一起工
作，他们互相扶助他们的
生命和财产。

青春的尼罗河

从如此小的起源生出
了第一个强有力的"国
家"来。

这算是沿着进步的道
上，前进了一大步。

这使埃及境内成了一个真能住人的地方。这
意思是无法律的杀害的终了。这保证人命比以前
有更大的安全，给部落中的较弱的分子一个生存
的机会。如今当绝对的无规律的景象只在阿非
利加丛林中存在时，这是难以想象的一个个无法
律警察，裁判官，卫生管理员，医院和学校的
世界。

但是五千年以前，只有埃及是有组织的国
家，大为邻人所嫉忌。这些邻人只能单手独臂地
周旋他们的生命的困难。

然而一个国家并非只有人民就可组成的。

那里必要有几个施行法律的人，如遇有紧急
之事时，还须有执行命令的人。惟一的元首，他

们或称王，或称皇帝，或称沙（如在波斯），或称总统（如我们本国所称呼的）。倘若没有元首，便没有一国能够持久了。

在古埃及，每一村落承认村之长者的威权，他们是老年人，较年幼者有更富的经验。这些长者选出一个壮健的人，以命令他们的兵士，如遇战争时，并在有大水时，吩咐他们做什么。他们给他一个尊称以便跟别人有所区别。他们称他为王或者君，服从他的命令，为他们自己的共同的利益。

所以在埃及，史的最初期，我们从人民中寻出以下的分类：

大多数是农民。

他们的全体都是一般贫富。

他们被一个强有力的人管理着，他是他们军队中的总司令，他委任他们的审判官，他为共同的利益和安全建筑道路。

膏腴的山谷

他也是警察局的局

长，拿捉盗贼。

为这些可贵的服务的报答，他从各人收入定量的金钱，这叫作税。然而这些税的大部分并非属于王的个人的。它们是委托于他为共同的事业所用的金钱。

但是不久以后有一类新的人民，既非农民，又非国王，开始发展着。这新的一类普通称做贵族的，是居在元首和他的国民之间。

从那些初期的日子，它已经在各国的历史中出现，它已经在各国的发展中演了一大幕。

我得给你们试释，这类的贵族怎样从最平凡的日常生活的环境中发展出来，它为甚么已维持它自己到了此日，越过了各种的反对。

为了使我的故事十分清楚起见，我已经画了一张图画。

它显示给你们五个埃及的农场。这些农场的原主已在好多年好多年的以前迁进了埃及各人已占据了一片空地而住下，在那里种五谷，牧牛，养猪，并做无论何种凡使他们自己和他们的儿女生存所必须的事情。显然地他们有同样的生存的机会。

封建制度的原始

后来有一个人做了五个农场的主人们的领袖，而丝毫不犯法律的，得握了一切他们的牧场和牛栏。这是怎样发生的呢？

收割后的一日，鱼先生（你在图上的象形中看他的名字）遣他的装载五谷的船到孟斐斯镇卖他的货物给中埃及的居民。这齐巧是农人的丰年，鱼于他的麦得了不少的金钱。十天后这船回转了家乡，船主把他所收到的金钱，交给他的主人。

几星期后，麻雀先生，他的农场是在鱼的隔壁，运他的麦到最近的市场去。可怜的麻雀近几年来的运气很不好。但是他希望给他的一次五谷的厚利的交易，以补偿他的近来的损失。所以他已经等着，直到孟斐斯的麦价会得稍稍高一些。

那天早晨，克里特岛中的荒年的流传已经达到这村落。结果，埃及市场中的五谷已大涨其价格。

麻雀希望从这市场的突变得到厚利，他叫他

的船主赶快。

船主把他的船上的舵如此的笨拙，这船撞在石上，沉下去了，溺死了这同伴，他是被覆在船底下。

麻雀非但全失了他的五谷和船，并且还不得不给他的那溺死了的同伴的寡妻十块金子，以作抚恤。

真是不凑巧，麻雀先生已经担不起再受损失，灾祸偏偏在这时候发生。冬季将近，而他没有金钱为他的子女购大褂。他已迁延了购新的锄和铲这样的长久，那旧的全已坏了。他没有了种子可以种他的田。他是在无可奈何的境况中。

他一点也不喜欢他的邻人鱼先生，然而无法可想了。他必须去，必须低首下心地请求少数金钱的借款。

他去访候鱼，鱼先生说他要多少，很愿意借给他，不过要他些担保品来作抵押。

麻雀说"是"。他愿意将他自己的农场做抵押。

不幸的关于那农场的一切，鱼全知道。它已属于麻雀的家族好几代。但是现在主人的父亲已让他自己给一个腓尼基商人欺骗得很厉害，我买了他的一对"弗里家牛"（谁也不知这名字是什么意思），据说这是很善的种类，它只需些微的食料而做出如普通埃及牛之两倍多的工作。年老的农人相信了这欺骗者的假正经的言语。他买了这神奇的动物，大为他一切的邻人所嫉忌。

他们没有证实它们的效验。

它们很笨拙，很迟缓并且出奇的懒惰；在三星期中，它们得了一种神秘的病症死去。

年老的农人遭受了打击是如此的愤怒，他的财产的管理是被留给了他的儿子，他认真地工作，但是并没有大效果。

他的五谷和船的丧失是末了的祸源。

小麻雀不是饿死，便是请求他的邻人助他以借款，只有这两条路可走。

鱼很熟知他全邻人的生活（他是那一种人，并非因为他爱讲闲话，但是从没人知道这种消息怎样会巧妙地得来），并且详细地知道麻雀的家庭状况，他觉得尽可坚持着某种条件，麻雀在下列的条件之下，能有一切他所需要的金钱。他须应许他每年给鱼做工六星期，并且，无论什么时候他须让他自由进入他的田地。

麻雀并不愿意这些条件，但是时日渐短，而冬季快来，并且他的一家没有食物。

他是不得不接受了。自从那时以后，他和他的儿女没有他们以前一样的十分自由了。

他们并非真成了他们邻人的仆役或奴隶，但是他们自己的生活依赖于他的仁慈。他们在路上遇见鱼时，他们立在一旁说："早安，先生。"是否答他们是听鱼的便。

现在他有很多的水边的田亩，如以前的两倍之多。

他有更多的田地和更多的工人。他能比以前的几年种植更多的五谷。近村人是谈论着他在盖的新屋。他大概是被尊为多财的要人。

那年夏天的后期发生了未之前闻的事情。

下雨了。

最老的居民不能想出这样的事，但是足足下了两天大而不停的雨，已被每人所忘记了它的存在的小溪，突然变成了猛烈的急流。在午夜从山上传下来雷声，毁灭了这占着在山脚下的石地的农人的秋收。他的名字是杯。他也是已从几百的先于他的杯们承袭着他的田地。这毁坏几乎是无法恢复。杯需要五谷的新种子，而且立刻需要它。他已听见过麻雀的故事。他也恨得去求惠于那到处以狡猾的买卖者闻名的鱼。但是终究他到了鱼的家里，卑下地请求几升麦的借项。他应允了每年在鱼的田内做两个足月的工作，方才如愿以偿。

鱼现在甚是顺利。他的新屋已经落成；他想他已到了给他自己做一家之长的时候了。

有一农人刚住在对面，他有一个年轻的女儿。这农人的名字是刀。他是一个从容不迫的人；他不能给他的女儿一份丰盛的妆奁。

鱼去访候刀，告诉刀说，他不在乎金钱。他是富足，他愿意不要一钱地携这女儿去。虽然，刀得应许遗传他的田地给他的女婿，如其他死了。

事情照这样做了。

遗嘱是合法地在一个公证人前缮就；婚姻成立了，鱼现在有了（或者是近乎有）四个农场的大部分。

这是真的，有一第五块农场适居于余者之

中。但是名叫镰的产业，若不经过鱼所统辖的田地，不能运他的麦到市上去。再者，镰不是很有作为的，他愿意雇他自己于鱼，在他和他的老妻的日后的衣食住能得到供给的条件之下。他们没有儿女，这措置担保给他们以一安乐的晚年。当镰死时，一个远房的侄子出面，索取他伯父的农场的所有权。鱼放出狗去追逐他，那汉子便从没再见过。

这些事务已经延续至二十年。

杯、镰和麻雀家的后辈永没疑问地承受他们的地位。他们认老鱼做"老爷"，他们是多少依赖他的好意，如其他们要继续着生活。

这老人死时，传给他的儿子很多的田亩，和一个在他的紧邻中大有影响的地位。

小鱼像他的父亲。他是很能干的，并且有蓬勃的野心当上埃及王去征野性的柏柏族时，他自行去投诚。

他是打得如此地勇敢，王任命他做王家税务课的征收三百所村庄的税务官。

常时有某某农人不能付出他们的税。

于是小鱼姑且给他们一笔小借款。

在他们知道他的以前，他们是在给王家做征税员工作，以还他们所已借了的金钱和借款的利息。

一年年过去，鱼族无上地统辖了他们生长的地方。老家是最不适于给如此的要人住。

造了一个贵族院（照着底比斯的王家宴饮殿图样做的），一座高墙是建造着，阻挡着群众，让他们站得远远的，鱼如果没有带手枪的卫队随着他，他是永不出去的。

一年两次他到底比斯朝见他的王——他住在全埃及最大的王宫内，所以他是称做"法老""大厦"之所有者。

在他的某次朝见中，他带了鱼第三，这家族之创始者的孙子，他是一个美貌的少年。

法老的女儿看见了这少年，而欲得他做她的丈夫。婚礼用去了鱼大半的财产，但是他依旧是王家税务课的税务官，只要待人民残酷些，不到三年，他便能充满了他的保险箱。

当他死了，他是埋葬在一个小的金字塔中，正如他是王亲之一员，并有一法老的女儿在他的坟上哭。

那是我的故事，它开始于沿尼罗河畔之某处，它于三代中从一般卑下的祖先中提拔起一农人，而掷他于附近皇宫的金銮殿的门外。

所遭逢于鱼的，也遭逢于多数具有同等能干而有财力的人。

他们独自成为一类。

他们彼此娶彼此的女儿，这样他们使得家财握在少数的人手中。

他们忠心地为王服役，如他的军队中的将校和他的税务课中的税务员。

他们留意于街路和水道的安全。

他们成就了许多有用的事业，在他们自己中，他们服从高贵的条款，很严格的法律。

如其王是不良的，贵族也易于做不良的。

王柔弱时，贵族常打算把持这国家。

于是时常发生，人民从他们的激怒中起来，毁灭那些虐待他们的人。

许多的老贵族被杀死，田地重新划分，这给每人一个均等的机会。

但是不久以后，这老故事又亲自重复着。

这次或者是麻雀家族之一员，用他的巨猾和

实业使他自己成为一方之主（可贵的回忆），鱼之后裔降为贫穷。

其余的没有多大改变。

忠心的农人继续着做工而赋税。

同样忠心的税务官继续着谋财产。

但是古老的尼罗河——对有野心的人无所差别——如前一般镇静地在它的陈旧的两岸中流着，大公无私（这只能在自然力中寻到）地把它的丰饶的幸福嘉惠于贫人和富人。

VII. THE MAKING OF A STATE

NOWADAYS we all are members of a "state".

We may be Frenchmen or Chinamen or Russians; we may live in the furthest corner of Indonesia (do you know where that is), but in some way or other we belong to that curious combination of people which is called the "state".

It does not matter whether we recognize a king or an emperor or a president as our ruler. We are born and we die as a small part of this large Whole and no one can escape this fate.

The "state", as a matter of fact, is quite a recent invention.

The earliest inhabitants of the world did not know what it was.

Every family lived and hunted and worked and

died for and by itself. Sometimes it happened that a few of these families, for the sake of greater protection against the wild animals and against other wild people, formed a loose alliance which was called a tribe or a clan. But as soon as the danger was past, these groups of people acted again by and for themselves and if the weak could not defend their own cave, they were left to the mercies of the hyena and the tiger and nobody was very sorry if they were killed.

In short, each person was a nation unto himself and he felt no responsibility for the happiness and safety of his neighbor. Very, very slowly this was changed and Egypt was the first country where the people were organized into a well-regulated empire.

The Nile was directly responsible for this useful development. I have told you how in the summer of each year the greater part of the Nile valley and the Nile delta is turned into a vast inland sea. To derive the greatest benefit from this water and yet survive the flood, it had been necessary at certain points to build dykes and small islands which would offer shelter for man and beast during the months of August and September. The construction of these little artificial islands however had not been simple.

A single man or a single family or even a small tribe could not construct a river-dam without the help of others.

However much a farmer might dislike his neighbors he disliked getting drowned even more and he was obliged to call upon the entire country-side when the water of the river began to rise and threatened him and his wife and his children and his cattle with destruction.

Necessity forced the people to forget their small differences and soon the entire valley of the Nile was covered with little combinations of people who constantly worked together for a common purpose and who depended upon each other for life and prosperity.

Out of such small beginnings grew the first powerful State.

It was a great step forward along the road of progress.

It made the land of Egypt a truly inhabitable place. It meant the end of lawless murder. It assured the people greater safety than ever before and gave the weaker members of the tribe a chance to survive. Nowadays, when conditions of absolute disorder exist only in the jungles of Africa, it is hard to imagine a world without laws and policemen and judges and health officers and hospitals and schools.

But five thousand years ago, Egypt stood alone as an organized state and was greatly envied by those of her neighbors who were obliged to face the difficulties of life single-handedly.

A state, however, is not only composed of citizens.

There must be a few men who execute the laws and who, in case of an emergency, take command of the entire community. Therefore no country has ever been able to endure without a single head, be he called a King or an Emperor or a Shah (as in Persia) or a President, as he is called in our own land.

In ancient Egypt, every village recognized the authority of the Village-elders, who were old men and possessed greater experience than the young ones. These Elders selected a strong man to command their soldiers in case of war and to tell them what to do when there was a flood. They gave him a title which distinguished him from the others. They called him a King or a prince and obeyed his orders for their own common benefit.

Therefore in the oldest days of Egyptian history, we find the following division among the people:

The majority are peasants.

All of them are equally rich and equally poor.

They are ruled by a powerful man who is the commander-in-chief of their armies and who appoints their judges and causes roads to be built for the common benefit and comfort.

He also is the chief of the police force and catches the thieves.

In return for these valuable services he receives

a certain amount of everybody's money which is called a tax. The greater part of these taxes, however, do not belong to the King personally. They are money entrusted to him to be used for the common good.

But after a short while a new class of people, neither peasants nor king, begins to develop. This new class, commonly called the nobles, stands between the ruler and his subjects.

Since those early days it has made its appearance in the history of every country and it has played a great role in the development of every nation.

I must try and explain to you how this class of nobles developed out of the most commonplace circumstances of everyday life and why it has maintained itself to this very day, against every form of opposition.

To make my story quite clear, I have drawn a picture.

It shows you five Egyptian farms. The original owners of these farms had moved into Egypt years and years ago. Each had taken a piece of unoccupied land and had settled down upon it to raise grain and cows and pigs and do whatever was necessary to keep themselves and their children alive. Apparently they had the same chance in life.

How then did it happen that one became the ruler of his neighbors and got hold of all their fields and barns without breaking a single law?

One day after the harvest, Mr. Fish (you see his name in hieroglyphics on the map) sent his boat loaded with grain to the town of Memphis to sell the cargo to the inhabitants of central Egypt. It happened to have been a good year for the farmer and Fish got a great deal of money for his wheat. After ten days the boat returned to the homestead and the captain handed the money which he had received to his employer.

A few weeks later, Mr. Sparrow, whose farm was next to that of Fish, sent his wheat to the nearest market. Poor Sparrow had not been very lucky for the last few years. But he hoped to make up for his recent losses by a profitable sale of his grain. Therefore he had waited until the price of wheat in Memphis should have gone a little higher.

That morning a rumor had reached the village of a famine in the island of Crete. As a result the grain in the Egyptian markets had greatly increased in value.

Sparrow hoped to profit through this unexpected turn of the market and he bade his skipper to hurry.

The skipper handled the rudder of his craft so clumsily that the boat struck a rock and sank, drowning the mate who was caught under the sail.

Sparrow not only lost all his grain and his ship but he was also forced to pay the widow of his drowned mate ten pieces of gold to make up for the loss of her husband.

These disasters occurred at the very moment when Sparrow could not afford another loss.

Winter was near and he had no money to buy cloaks for his children. He had put off buying new hoes and spades for such a long time that the old ones were completely worn out. He had no seeds for his fields. He was in a desperate plight.

He did not like his neighbor, Mr. Fish, any too well but there was no way out. He must go and humbly he must ask for the loan of a small sum of money.

He called on Fish. The latter said that he would gladly let him have whatever he needed but could Sparrow put up any sort of guaranty?

Sparrow said, "Yes." He would offer his own farm as a pledge of good faith.

Unfortunately Fish knew all about that farm. It had belonged to the Sparrow family for many generations. But the Father of the present owner had allowed himself to be terribly cheated by a Phoenician trader who had sold him a couple of "Phrygian Oxen" (nobody knew what the name meant) which were said to be of a very fine breed, which needed little food and performed twice as much labor as the common Egyptian oxen. The old farmer had believed the solemn words of the impostor. He had bought the wonderful beasts, greatly envied by all his neighbors.

They had not proved a success.

They were very stupid and very slow and exceedingly lazy and within three weeks they had died from a mysterious disease.

The old farmer was so angry that he suffered a stroke and the management of his estate was left to the son, who worked hard but without much result.

The loss of his grain and his vessel were the last straw.

Young Sparrow must either starve or ask his neighbor to help him with a loan.

Fish who was familiar with the lives of all his neighbors (he was that kind of person, not because he loved gossip but one never knew how such information might come in handy) and who knew to a penny the state of affairs in the Sparrow household, felt strong enough to insist upon certain terms. Sparrow could have all the money he needed upon the following condition. He must promise to work for Fish six weeks of every year and he must allow him free access to his grounds at all times.

Sparrow did not like these terms, but the days were growing shorter and winter was coming on fast and his family were without food.

He was forced to accept and from that time on, he and his sons and daughters were no longer quite as free as they had been before.

They did not exactly become the servants or the slaves of their neighbor, but they were dependent upon his kindness for their own livelihood. When they met Fish in the road they stepped aside and said, "Good morning, sir." And he answered them—or not—as the case might be.

He now owned a great deal of water-front, twice as much as before.

He had more land and more laborers and he could raise more grain than in the past years. The nearby villagers talked of the new house he was building and in a general way, he was regarded as a man of growing wealth and importance.

Late that summer an unheard-of-thing happened.

It rained.

The oldest inhabitants could not remember such a thing, but it rained hard and steadily for two whole days. A little brook, the existence of which everybody had forgotten, was suddenly turned into a wild torrent. In the middle of the night it came thundering down from the mountains and destroyed the harvest of the farmer who occupied the rocky ground at the foot of the hills. His name was Cup and he too had inherited his land from a hundred other Cups who had gone before. The damage was almost irreparable. Cup needed new seed grain and he needed it at once. He had heard Sparrow's story. He too hated to ask a favor of Fish who was known far and wide as a shrewd dealer. But in the end, he found his way to the Fishes' homestead and humbly begged for the loan of a few bushels of wheat. He got them but not until he had agreed to work two whole months of each year on the farm of Fish.

Fish was now doing very well. His new house was ready and he thought the time had come to establish himself as the head of a household.

Just across the way, there lived a farmer who had a young daughter. The name of this farmer was Knife. He was a happy-go-lucky person and he could not give his child a large dowry.

Fish called on Knife and told him that he did not care for money. He was rich and he was willing to take the daughter without a single penny. Knife, however, must promise to leave his land to his son-in-law in case he died.

This was done.

The will was duly drawn up before a notary, the wedding took place and Fish now possessed (or was about to possess) the greater part of four farms.

It is true there was a fifth farm situated right in between the others. But its owner, by the name of Sickle, could not carry his wheat to the market without crossing the lands over which Fish held sway. Besides, Sickle was not very energetic and he willingly hired himself out to Fish on condition that he and his old wife be given a room and food and clothes for the rest of their days. They had no children and this settlement assured them a peaceful old age. When Sickle died, a distant nephew appeared who claimed a right to his uncle's farm. Fish had the dogs turned loose on him and the fellow was never seen again.

These transactions had covered a period of twenty years.

The younger generations of the Cup, Sickle and Sparrow families accepted their situation in life without questioning. They knew old Fish as "the Squire" upon whose good-will they were more or less dependent if they wanted to succeed in life.

When the old man died he left his son many wide acres and a position of great influence among his immediate neighbors.

Young Fish resembled his father. He was very able and had a great deal of ambition. When the king of Upper Egypt went to war against the wild Berber tribes, he volunteered his services.

He fought so bravely that the king appointed him

Collector of the Royal Revenue for three hundred villages.

Often it happened that certain farmers could not pay their tax.

Then young Fish offered to give them a small loan.

Before they knew it, they were working for the Royal Tax Gatherer, to repay both the money which they had borrowed and the interest on the loan.

The years went by and the Fish family reigned supreme in the land of their birth. The old home was no longer good enough for such important people.

A noble hall was built (after the pattern of the Royal Banqueting Hall of Thebes). A high wall was erected to keep the crowd at a respectful distance and Fish never went out without a bodyguard of armed soldiers.

Twice a year he travelled to Thebes to be with his King, who lived in the largest palace of all Egypt and who was therefore known as "Pharaoh", the owner of the "Big House".

Upon one of his visits, he took Fish the Third, grandson of the founder of the family, who was a handsome young fellow.

The daughter of Pharaoh saw the youth and desired him for her husband. The wedding cost Fish most of his fortune, but he was still Collector of the Royal Revenue and by treating the people without mercy he was able to fill his strong-box in less than three years.

When he died he was buried in a small Pyramid, just as if he had been a member of the Royal Family, and a daughter of Pharaoh wept over his grave.

That is my story which begins somewhere along the banks of the Nile and which in the course of three generations lifts a farmer from the ranks of his own humble ancestors and drops him outside the gate but near the throne-room of the King's palace.

What happened to Fish, happened to a large number of equally energetic and resourceful men.

They formed a class apart.

They married each other's daughters and in this

way they kept the family fortunes in the hands of a small number of people.

They served the King faithfully as officers in his army and as collectors of his taxes.

They looked after the safety of the roads and the waterways.

They performed many useful tasks and among themselves they obeyed the laws of a very strict code of honor.

If the Kings were bad, the nobles were apt to be bad too.

When the Kings were weak the nobles often managed to get hold of the State.

Then it often happened that the people arose in their wrath and destroyed those who oppressed them.

Many of the old nobles were killed and a new division of the land took place which gave everybody an equal chance.

But after a short while the old story repeated itself.

This time it was perhaps a member of the Sparrow

family who used his greater shrewdness and industry to make himself master of the countryside while the descendants of Fish (of glorious memory) were reduced to poverty.

Otherwise very little was changed.

The faithful peasants continued to work and pay taxes.

The equally faithful tax gatherers continued to gather wealth.

But the old Nile, indifferent to the ambitions of men, flowed as placidly as ever between its age-worn banks and bestowed its fertile blessings upon the poor and upon the rich with the impartial justice which is found only in the forces of nature.

八　埃及的兴起和倾覆

我们常听见说"文化西渐"。我们所说的意思，就是那刚毅的开辟者，已经渡过了大西洋而散居在沿新英格兰和新尼德兰之边——就是他们的儿女们已经走过了广漠的旷野——就是他们的曾孙们已迁进了加利福尼亚——就是本代的子孙希望广漠的太平洋改变成时代之最重要的洋海。

实在的，"文化"永不会老守在同一地点。它是常到别处去，但是它终究并非老是向着西行的。有时它的行程是向着东或者南。它常时在地图上曲折进行的。然而它是终不止息。在二三百年后文化似乎说，"得啦，我已跟这族人伴得够久了。"它便包扎了它的书籍，它的科学，它的艺术和它的音乐，而向前徘徊以寻觅新的领土。但是没有一人知道它往何处去，那使它的生活如此有趣味的是什么。

在埃及的情形，文化之中心是沿尼罗河岸的

膏腴山谷的土壤

南北向移动着。

最初我已对你们说过，人民是从阿非利加和西亚细亚的各处迁进了这流域而住下。由是他们组成了小的村和镇；领受了总司令的管辖，他是叫作法老，在下埃及的孟斐斯有他的首都。

二千年后，这老家的元首渐渐弱得再不能维持他们自己了。有一个新的家族。从上埃及的朝南三百五十哩的底比斯出来，想使它自己做全流域之主。纪元前二千四百年，他们成功了。做了上下埃及的元首，他们出发去克服世界的其余的部分。他们向着尼罗河源（这地方他们从来没有达到）行进，征服了爱西屋皮亚黑人。次之，他们经过了赛奈的沙漠而侵袭叙利亚，在那里他们使得他们的名声给巴比伦人和亚西利亚人所惧怕着。有了这些远离的区域，保证了埃及的安全。他们能为凡能住在那里的一切的人，将这流域改造成一个快乐地。他们筑了许多新的堤坝和水闻，并在沙漠中造了一个广大的蓄水池，在这里面他们贮满了尼罗河的水，以备久旱时应用，他们鼓励人民献他们自己于研读数学和天文，因此他们可以推知尼罗河的泛滥想要来了的时候。因为为了这目的，一个巧妙的，用此能计算时期的法子，是必要的，他们制定三百六十五日为一年，他们分它做十二月。

使埃及人同一切外国物件相隔的古老的习俗相反，他们让埃及的货品与从无论何处已带进了他们的海口的东西相交换。

他们跟克里特的希腊人和西亚细亚的阿剌伯人通商；他们从印度得到香料，从中国输入金子和丝绸。

但是一切的人的组织都是服从某种进步和退化的定律，国家或朝代也没有例外。经过四百年的茂盛后，这些强有力的王渐呈疲惫的现象。这些大埃及帝国的元首与其骑在骆驼上做他们的军队的领袖，宁可登在他们的宫殿中听筝或笛的音乐。

一日有流传来到底比斯城说，马队的野族已在沿边界劫掠。于是埃及国王派出一支军队去驱逐他们，这支军队行进沙漠，竟被凶狠的阿剌伯人杀得一个不留。于是亚剌伯人向尼罗河进攻，抢去了埃及人的羊群和他们的家用什物。

埃及王又遣一支军队去阻止他们的进行。这战争是致祸于埃及人，尼罗河流域的门是对侵袭者开着。

他们骑的是快马，用的是弓和箭，在极短的时间内，他们已使他们自己做了全国之主。他们统辖了埃及五世纪。他们迁这古都到尼罗河的三角洲。

他们虐待埃及农人。

他们很凶地待遇大人，他们杀戮小孩，他们对古神是粗暴的。他们不喜欢住在城内，只是同他们的羊群登在旷野中，所以他们是叫作喜克索，这意思是"牧羊的王"。

到底他们的管理渐成了不能再忍受的了。

有一底比斯城的贵族自做了对外国的霸占者的国内革民的领袖。这是不很有望的战争，然而埃及人得胜了。喜克索是被逐出国境，他们回到那他们从那里来的沙漠去。经验做了给埃及人的警告。他们的五百年的外国奴隶是一可惊的经验。这种事情必得永不再发生。祖国的边界必须弄得坚固的没有一人再敢来袭击这圣地。

一个新的底比斯王，名替摩雪斯的，侵袭了亚细亚，而且他再也不停，直至他达到了美索不达迷亚的平原。他饮他的牛于幼发拉的河；巴比伦和尼尼微一提到他的名字便惊恐。无论何处他所去了的，他筑着坚固的堡垒，且以优美的道路连接着。已筑好了一防御未来的侵袭的堡栅，替摩雪斯回家而死了。但是他的女儿，哈兹塞脱，继续他的善美的工作。她重造喜克索所已毁灭了的庙宇；她建设了一个坚强的国家，在它的下面，兵士和商人为共同的目的一起工作，它是叫作新帝国，持续了从纪元前一千六百年到一千三百年。

然而军治的国家终不能持续得很久。国家越大，需要为它防御的人越多；军队中的人越多，能住家种田和行商的人越少。在几年中，埃及国已成了头重脚轻的了；军队，这是防御外国侵袭的堡垒的意思，从人工和金钱的两俱缺乏，将国家拖入了倾覆中。

毫无阻碍从亚细亚来的野民是在袭击那些坚

固的堡栅，在这后面埃及藏着全文化界的富源。

起初埃及的卫戍兵还能保守他们自己的地位。

然而，一日，在远离的美索不达迷亚，有一新的军治帝国起来，这叫作亚细利亚。它既不注重艺术，也不留意科学，但是它能战争。亚细利亚人向埃及进军，而在战争中将他们打败了。他们统治了尼罗河地方二十余年。这对埃及的意思是终局的开端。

有几次，短时间的，这人民设法重得了他们的独立。但是，他们是老种族了；他们是给几世纪来的艰苦的工作消磨尽了。

这时他们从历史舞台上退出，而投出他们做世界上最进化的民族的领袖的降表的时候已经来临。希腊商人是群集于尼罗河口之城市中。

新都是建筑这舍易斯，近尼罗河口，埃及成了一个纯粹的商业国家，西亚细亚和东欧罗巴之贸易的中心点。

继希腊人而来的是波斯人，他们征服了北阿非利加的全部。

二世纪后，大亚历山大将法老的古地改做希

腊的一省。他死后，他的将军之一，名叫托勒密的，立他自己做新埃及国的独立的王。

托勒密的家族继续着统治了二百年。

纪元前的三十年，托勒密氏之末一位克利奥佩特剌杀了她自己，强于做凯旋的罗马将军，屋大威纳斯的俘虏。

那是终局。

埃及成了罗马帝国的一部分；她的独立国家的生命便永远停止了。

VIII. THE RISE AND FALL OF EGYPT

WE often hear it said that "civilization travels westward". What we mean is that hardy pioneers have crossed the Atlantic Ocean and settled along the shores of New England and New Netherland—that their children have crossed the vast prairies—that their great-grandchildren have moved into California—and that the present generation hopes to turn the vast Pacific into the most important sea of the ages.

As a matter of fact, "civilization" never remains long in the same spot. It is always going somewhere but it does not always move westward by any means. Sometimes its course points towards the east or the south. Often it zigzags across the map. But it keeps moving. After two or three hundred years, civilization seems to say, "Well, I have been keeping company with these particular people long enough," and it packs its books and its science and its art and its music, and wanders forth in search of new domains. But no one knows whither it is bound, and that is what makes life so interesting.

In the case of Egypt, the center of civilization moved northward and southward, along the banks of the Nile. First of all, as I told you, people from all over Africa and western Asia moved into the valley and settled down. Thereupon they formed small villages and townships and accepted the rule of a Commander-in-chief, who was called Pharaoh, and who had his capital in Memphis, in the lower part of Egypt.

After a couple of thousand years, the rulers of this ancient house became too weak to maintain themselves. A new family from the town of Thebes, 350 miles towards the south in Upper Egypt, tried to make itself master of the entire valley. In the year 2400 B.C. they succeeded. As rulers of both

Upper and Lower Egypt, they set forth to conquer
the rest of the world. They marched towards the
sources of the Nile (which they never reached) and
conquered black Ethiopia. Next they crossed the
desert of Sinai and invaded Syria where they made
their name feared by the Babylonians and Assyrians.
The possession of these outlying districts assured
the safety of Egypt and they could set to work to
turn the valley into a happy home, for as many of
the people as could find room there. They built
many new dikes and dams and a vast reservoir in
the desert which they filled with water from the Nile
to be kept and used in case of a prolonged drought.
They encouraged people to devote themselves to the
study of mathematics and astronomy so that they
might determine the time when the floods of the Nile
were to be expected. Since for this purpose it was
necessary to have a handy method by which time
could be measured, they established the year of 365
days, which they divided into twelve months.

Contrary to the old tradition which made the

Egyptians keep away from all things foreign, they allowed the exchange of Egyptian merchandise for goods which had been carried to their harbors from elsewhere.

They traded with the Greeks of Crete and with the Arabs of western Asia and they got spices from the Indies and they imported gold and silk from China.

But all human institutions are subject to certain definite laws of progress and decline and a State or a dynasty is no exception. After four hundred years of prosperity, these mighty kings showed signs of growing tired. Rather than ride a camel at the head of their army, the rulers of the great Egyptian Empire stayed within the gates of their palace and listened to the music of the harp or the flute.

One day there came rumors to the town of Thebes that wild tribes of horsemen had been pillaging along the frontiers. An army was sent to drive them away. This army moved into the desert. To the last man it was killed by the fierce Arabs, who now marched towards the Nile, bringing their flocks of sheep and their household goods.

Another army was told to stop their progress. The battle was disastrous for the Egyptians and the valley of the Nile was open to the invaders.

They rode fleet horses and they used bows and arrows. Within a short time they had made themselves master of the entire country. For five centuries they ruled the land of Egypt. They removed the old capital to the Delta of the Nile.

They oppressed the Egyptian peasants.

They treated the men cruelly and they killed the children and they were rude to the ancient gods. They did not like to live in the cities but stayed with their flocks in the open fields and therefore they were called the Hyksos, which means the Shepherd Kings.

At last their rule grew unbearable.

A noble family from the city of Thebes placed itself at the head of a national revolution against the foreign usurpers. It was a desperate fight but the Egyptians won. The Hyksos were driven out of the country, and they went back to the desert whence they had come. The experience had been a warning to the Egyptian people. Their five hundred years of foreign slavery had been a terrible experience. Such a thing must never happen again. The frontier of the fatherland must be made so strong that no one dare to attack the holy soil.

A new Theban king, called Tethmosis, invaded Asia and never stopped until he reached the plains of Mesopotamia. He watered his oxen in the river Euphrates, and Babylon and Nineveh trembled at the mention of his name. Wherever he went, he built strong fortresses, which were connected by excellent roads. Tethmosis, having built a barrier against future invasions, went home and died. But his daughter, Hatshepsut, continued his good work. She rebuilt the temples which the Hyksos had destroyed and she founded a strong state in which soldiers and merchants worked together for a common purpose and which was called the New Empire, and lasted from 1600 to 1300 B.C.

Military nations, however, never last very long.

The larger the empire, the more men are needed for its defense and the more men there are in the army, the fewer can stay at home to work the farms and attend to the demands of trade. Within a few years, the Egyptian state had become top-heavy and the army, which was meant to be a bulwark against foreign invasion, dragged the country into ruin from sheer lack of both men and money.

Without interruption, wild people from Asia were attacking those strong walls behind which Egypt was hoarding the riches of the entire civilized world.

At first the Egyptian garrisons could hold their own.

One day, however, in distant Mesopotamia, there arose a new military empire which was called Assyria. It cared for neither art nor science, but it could fight. The Assyrians marched against the Egyptians and defeated them in battle. For more than twenty years they ruled the land of the Nile. To Egypt this meant the beginning of the end.

A few times, for short periods, the people

managed to regain their independence. But they were an old race, and they were worn out by centuries of hard work.

The time had come for them to disappear from the stage of history and surrender their leadership as the most civilized people of the world. Greek merchants were swarming down upon the cities at the mouth of the Nile.

A new capital was built at Sais, near the mouth of the Nile, and Egypt became a purely commercial state, the half-way house for the trade between western Asia and eastern Europe.

After the Greeks came the Persians, who conquered all of northern Africa.

Two centuries later, Alexander the Great turned the ancient land of the Pharaoh into a Greek province. When he died, one of his generals, Ptolemy by name, established himself as the independent king of a new Egyptian state.

The Ptolemy family continued to rule for two hundred years.

In the year 30 B.C., Cleopatra, the last of the Ptolemys, killed herself, rather than become a prisoner of the victorious Roman general, Octavianus.

That was the end.

Egypt became part of the Roman Empire and her life as an independent state ceased for all time.

九　美索不达迷亚①
——两河之间的陆地

我再带你们到最高的金字塔之顶上去。

登上去是要攀援重攀援的。

在起初建筑这人工之山时，是用粗糙的花岗石垒成的。再在花岗石上加上一层精美的石头。但现今这层精美的石头是早已损坏或是被人家窃去，建造新的罗马城市去了。一只山羊也得要有很多的时间爬上这奇峰。但是得了几个阿剌伯小孩的帮助，我们在几小时的坚忍的工作后，就可以达到顶上了；在那里我们可以休息而遥观到人类的历史的第二章。

在辽远的辽远的广漠之沙漠的黄沙以外，老尼罗河即从中经过以通至海的，你会看见（如其你有鹞鹰的眼睛）些光闪闪的碧碧绿的东西。

---

① 通译为美索不达米亚。

　　这是一个介乎两大河之间的山谷。

　　这是在古地图上最有趣的一点。

　　这是《旧约》的极乐园。

　　这是神秘和奇妙的古地，希腊人叫它做美索不达迷亚。

　　"Mesos"一字的意思是"中间"或"在二者之间"，而"potomos"是希腊语的河。只要想想hippopotamus（河马），生在河中的马或"hippos"。所以美索不达迷亚是一带"在两河之间"的地方的意思。这里的两河是幼发拉的，叫它做"浦剌都"和底格里斯。巴比伦人叫它做"狄克拉忒"。你会从地图上看见它们俩。它们发源于亚美尼亚（Armenia）的北山之雪中；它们慢慢地流过南平原而直达波斯湾的泥污的岸。但是在它们失掉它们自己于这印度洋之支流的波浪中以前，它们已成就了一个伟大而有用的工作。

　　它们已将一非常干燥的区域，改变成西亚细亚唯一的肥沃的地方。

　　那种事实会给你释明为何美索不达迷亚跟北山和南沙漠的居民如此的投机。

　　这是一件显明的事实，就是一切的生物全欢

喜适意。下雨的时候，猫赶速地避到有庇荫的地方。

天冷时，狗在火炉前寻一席地。在海之某部成为较以前更咸（或更淡，看当时的情形）时，无数的小鱼快快游到汪洋之别一部去。至于鸟，它们中有许多照例地每年一次从此处迁到彼处。冷天开始时，雁鹅飞去，而当第一只燕子飞回来时，我们知道那夏日大约要对我们微笑了。

人并不是这个定律的例外。他喜欢温暖的火炉更甚于冷风。无论何时，他于选择一餐美馔和一块面包皮之间，他是宁取美馔的。如其这是绝对的必需时，他会住在沙漠中或北极带的寒雪中。但是供他一较适宜的居留地时，他会毫不踌躇地接受了。这改进他的地位的愿望，真的使他的生活更安适而减疲惫的意思是愿望，于世界的进步是件很好的东西。

它已驱欧罗巴的白人至地球的两端。

它已殖民于我们本国的山上和平原上。

它已使几百万人不息地从东到西，从南到北游行，直到他们找到了一个气候和生活状况于他们最合适的地方。

在亚细亚的西部，这迫生物用最少的工作的耗费力以尽力寻求更丰富的安适的本能，使得住在寒冷而荒芜的山上的居民，和住在焦灼的沙漠中的人民，不得不在美索不达迷亚的幸福的山谷中寻一新的居留地。

这使得他们战争，为了要专有这尘世的天堂。

这逼得他们操练他们是最高的创造力和可贵的坚毅，以防御他们的家室农场，妻子和儿女于新来者，他们是世世纪纪的被这快乐地的名声摄引来。

这不断的逐鹿是这族，老而已定了基业的，和别族为他们的染指想夺取地土的，永远竞争着的缘由。

那些柔弱的和那些并没充分之精力的少有成功的机会。

只有最有智力而最勇敢的存留着。那会给你解释明白为何美索不达迷亚成了一族健壮之人的家乡，能建设着那文化的国家，这文化给了一切的后代如此无限的利益。

IX. MESOPOTAMIA, THE COUNTRY BETWEEN THE RIVERS

I am going to take you to the top of the highest pyramid.

It is a good deal of a climb.

The casing of fine stones which in the beginning covered the rough granite blocks which were used to construct this artificial mountain, has long since worn off or has been stolen to help build new Roman cities. A goat would have a fine time scaling this strange peak. But with the help of a few Arab boys, we can get to the top after a few hours of hard work, and there we can rest and look far into the next chapter of the history of the human race.

Way, way off, in the distance, far beyond the yellow sands of the vast desert, through which the old Nile had cut herself a way to the sea, you will (if you have the eyes of a hawk), see something shimmering and green.

It is a valley situated between two big rivers.

It is the most interesting spot of the ancient map.

It is the Paradise of the Old Testament.

It is the old land of mystery and wonder which the Greeks called Mesopotamia.

The word "Mesos" means "middle" or "in between" and "potomos" is the Greek expression for river. (Just think of the Hippopotamus, the horse or "hippos" that lives in the rivers.) Mesopotamia, therefore, meant a stretch of land "between the rivers". The two rivers in this case were the Euphrates which the Babylonians called the "Purattu" and the Tigris, which the Babylonians called the "Diklat". You will see them both upon the map. They begin their course amidst the snows of the northern mountains of Armenia and slowly they flow through the southern plain until they reach the muddy banks of the Persian Gulf. But before they have lost themselves amidst the waves of this branch of the Indian Ocean, they have performed a great and useful task.

They have turned an otherwise arid and dry region into the only fertile spot of western Asia.

That fact will explain to you why Mesopotamia was so very popular with the inhabitants of the northern mountains and the southern desert.

It is a well-known fact that all living beings like to be comfortable. When it rains, the cat hastens to a place of shelter.

When it is cold, the dog finds a spot in front of the stove. When a certain part of the sea becomes more salty than it has been before (or less, for that matter) myriads of little fishes swim hastily to another part of the wide ocean. As for the birds, a great many of them move from one place to another regularly once a year. When the cold weather sets in, the geese depart, and when the first swallow returns, we know that summer is about to smile upon us.

Man is no exception to this rule. He likes

the warm stove much better than the cold wind. Whenever he has the choice between a good dinner and a crust of bread, he prefers the dinner. He will live in the desert or in the snow of the arctic zone if it is absolutely necessary. But offer him a more agreeable place of residence and he will accept without a moment's hesitation. This desire to improve his condition, which really means a desire to make life more comfortable and less wearisome, has been a very good thing for the progress of the world.

It has driven the white people of Europe to the ends of the earth.

It has populated the mountains and the plains of our own country.

It has made many millions of men travel ceaselessly from east to west and from south to north until they have found the climate and the living conditions which suit them best.

In the western part of Asia this instinct which compels living beings to seek the greatest amount of comfort possible with the smallest expenditure of labor forced both the inhabitants of the cold and inhospitable mountains and the people of the parched desert to look for a new dwelling place in the happy valley of Mesopotamia.

It caused them to fight for the sole possession of this Paradise upon Earth.

It forced them to exercise their highest power of inventiveness and their noblest courage to defend their homes and farms and their wives and children against the newcomers, who century after century were attracted by the fame of this pleasant spot.

This constant rivalry was the cause of an everlasting struggle between the old and established tribes and the others who clamored for their share of the soil.

Those who were weak and those who did not have a great deal of energy had little chance of success.

Only the most intelligent and the bravest survived. That will explain to you why Mesopotamia became the home of a strong race of men, capable of creating that state of civilization which was to be of such enormous benefit to all later generations.

十　萨谟利亚人的楔形文字

　　在哥伦布发现亚美利加不久以前的一千四百七十二年，有一名叫约瑟反巴巴洛的威尼西亚人遍游波斯，路经附近设刺子的山，看见了些使他难以索解的东西。设刺子山上是满布着旧庙宇，这些庙宇是刻凿在山旁的岩石中。古代的崇拜者已不见于几世纪的以前；庙宇是在大毁坏的景况中。但是在它们的墙壁上清楚地可见的，巴巴洛观察着用古怪的文体所写的长的稗史，这似乎是用尖钉所刻的一组的裂痕。

　　他回来后，他在他的乡友面前，陈述他的发现，但是正在那时，土耳其人恫吓欧罗巴以侵袭，人民是无暇于为了西亚细亚之中心的某处的一种新而不懂的字母有所纷扰。因此，波斯的刻文立被忘却了。

　　两世纪半以后，有一名叫皮亚屈罗但拉发勒的罗马少年贵族，游访这巴巴洛已在二百年以前经过的同一的设剌子的山坡。他也是无从索解这残壁上的奇特的刻文；他是一个精细的少年，谨慎地抄了它们，附了些关于这次旅行的记录寄他的报告给他的一个朋友斯岐佩拿医生，他在那不勒斯实习医学，而且此外他还有志于学问。

斯岐佩拿抄了这可笑的小的图像，引招它们给别的研究科学的人的注意。不幸地欧罗巴又给别的事务占去了。

可惊的普洛忒斯敦人和卡托利人间的战争已突然发生，人民是在忙于杀那些在宗教界中的某几点不跟他们相符合的人。

在能切实地着手研究楔样的刻文以前，又过去了一世纪。

第十八世纪——灵敏而有奇思的人的愉乐期——是爱好索解科学的疑难之谜的，所以当丹麦的腓特烈王五世征求加入他打算遣往西亚细亚的远探队的学者时，他得到了无穷的应征者。他的远探队，这在一千七百六十一年离别哥本哈根，持续了六年。在这期间内除了一个名叫卡斯腾尼布尔的以外，一切的队员全死了，他本是一个日耳曼的农人，能够忍受艰辛，比那些终日钻在他们藏书室的干燥的书堆中的教授们更能吃苦。

这尼布尔，他的职司是考察，是一个年轻的人，他是我们应得叹服的。

他一径独自地继续着他的行程，直至他到了百泄波里的残墟，在那里他费了一月的工夫，抄着所能寻见的在那倾覆了的宫殿和庙宇的墙壁上的每一个刻文。

他回转丹麦后，为了科学界的便利，他刊行了他的发现；他切实地试欲从他自己的原文中解悟些意义。

他没有成功。

但是这个工作本来是很困难的，所以虽是没有成功，我们也不惊讶。

善波力温攫得了古埃及的象形文时，他便能从小的图像作他的研究。

百泄波里的字体绝不显示任何的图像。

它们是由那无穷地重复着的 V 样的图形所组织成的，这对欧罗巴人的眼睛一些都启示不了什么。

如今，当这难题已给解明了，我们知道萨谟

利亚人的原文是一种图形文字，适跟埃及人的一样。

模形文字的刻石

但是，虽然埃及人在极早的日子已发现了纸草片，能描写他们的图像于光滑的平面上，美索不达迷亚的居民只能刻他们的言语在山旁的坚石或软的泥砖之中。

为必须所驱，他们已单纯化了原来的图像，直至他们计划出一种五百余不同的字之结构的组织，这是为他们的需要所必须的了。

让我给你们几个例。在起初，一颗星，用钉子画在砖中的，类乎下面的 ✳ 。

但是一回后，这星的样子因是太繁琐而被弃了，定这图像的样子是这样 ✳ 。

不久后"天"的意义加上于"星"的，这图像单纯化作这样 ↦ ，这使的它更难索解了。

用同样的法子一头牛从 ᖱ 改变成 ✙ 。

一尾鱼从 ᖰ 改变成 ✤ 。太阳，本来是一平面的圆圈的，变成了 ᕤ 。如其今日我们是在用萨谟利亚的字体，我们要作 🔑 如 🗝 。

你会明白揣摩这些图像的意义是怎样的困难，但是名叫格洛忒分特的日耳曼教师的坚忍的工作，终究得到了酬报；尼布尔的原文第一次发行后的三十年和楔样的图像第一次发现后的三世纪，四个字母已被阐明了。

这四个字母是 D，A，R 和 Sh。

它们拼成 Darheush 王的名字，我们称他做达理阿。

于是遭逢了只能在那些电报线和邮政汽船已将全世界变成了一大城市的以前的愉快日子所遭逢的事中之一件。

当坚忍的欧罗巴的教授们在燃着了午夜之烛，以图解明他们的新的亚细亚的神秘时，年少的亨利罗灵逊是在度他的不列颠东印度军队的武备学生的学年。

他用他的余暇的时间学习波斯文，在波斯的沙乞假少数的将校以训练他的本国的军队，于英吉利政府时，罗灵逊是被命至德黑兰去。他旅行遍了波斯，一日他偶访贝希斯敦村。波斯人叫它做巴吉斯坦那，这意思是"神祇之居处"。

数世纪前，这自美索不达迷亚至伊兰（波斯人的老家）的大道已通过这村落，而且波斯王达理阿已用了高耸的悬崖之陡峻的城墙，以宣告于全世界，他是何其伟大的人。

路旁的高头，他雕刻着他的显赫的伟业的记录。

这刻文是刻着波斯言语，巴比伦文和苏萨城的方言。使这故事明白于一些也不能读的那些人起见，加上了一幅显示波斯王置他的胜利的足于高马塔（尝想窃取王位于嫡传的元首的霸占者）的身上的佳妙的雕刻。为便利度量计，加着一打高马塔的跟从者。他们站在后面。他们的手是被绑着，他们不久便会被处决。

这图画和三种文字是在街道的上面几百尺，但是罗灵逊冒了生命和折肢的大险，爬上岩石的城墙上去而抄了这全文。

他的发现是最重要的。贝希斯敦石成了跟罗塞达石一样地有名，罗灵逊跟格洛忒分特共享阐明这古老的钉刻文的荣誉。

虽然他们从未看见过彼此或者听见过彼此的名字，这日耳曼教师和不列颠将校为共同的目

的合作着，如一切的善良的研究科学的人所当
做的。

他们的古文的抄本是在各地重印着，在十九
世纪的中叶，这楔形文字，所以这样称者，因为
这字母是楔的形式，"cuneus"是楔的拉丁名字）
已献出了它的秘密。又一人类的神秘已被解决。

但是对于已发明了这种技巧的字体之式样的
人民，我们终不能得知的很清楚。

他们是白种，他们称做萨谟利亚人。

他们住在我们叫它做叔麦的地方，他们自己
叫它做垦基，这意思是"芦之国"，这指示我们
他们尝住在美索不达迷亚山谷的卑湿区中。

原来萨谟利亚人是山居之民，后来他们被肥
泽的田地从山谷引诱了出来，但是当他们已离别
了在西亚细亚山峰中的古屋时，他们没有放弃了
他们的旧习惯，其中的一样，对我们有特殊的
趣味。

住在西亚细亚的山峰中，他们敬拜他们的上
帝于竖立在岩石顶上的祭坛上。在他们的新家，
在平原之中，那里没有这样的岩石，如旧样地建
筑他们的神岩是不可能。萨谟利亚人并不喜欢

如此。

一切的亚细亚人于习俗都有深深的缱绻，萨谟利亚人的习俗所要求的是一可在周围数哩彰明地看见的祭坛。

为克服这种艰难而保全他们跟他们的天爷上帝的平安计，萨谟利亚人建了一簇低塔（宛如小山），在那上面他们燃了他们的圣火以崇奉他们的旧时的上帝。

当犹太人去访游巴布伊利城（我们叫它做巴比伦）时——在末了的萨谟利亚人已死了数世纪后，他们深被高竖在美索不达迷亚的绿原中的奇观之塔感动着。巴别塔，我们常从《旧约》中听到它，不过是一座人工的山峰的残迹，在几百年前为一辈敬畏上帝的萨谟利亚人所建。这是一样奇异的计划物。

萨谟利亚人还不知道建造扶梯。

他们建一斜坡的走廊，环绕他们的塔，这渐渐地携人民从塔底至塔顶。

数年前这是觉得必须在纽约城的中心造一仿此的新的火车站，就是几千的旅客能在同一的时候从下层达到上层。

巴别塔

用扶梯想来是不安全的，因为如其有怒冲或者着了惊的民众必得滚下去，而那便成了骇人的灾祸。

工程师为了免除这种灾祸，便抄袭了萨谟利亚人的计划。

大中央站也置备着上升走廊，与三千年前初被采用于美索不达迷亚的平原中的一般。

X. THE SUMERIAN
NAIL WRITERS

IN the year 1472, a short time before Columbus discovered America, a certain Venetian, by the name of Josaphat Barbaro, traveling through Persia, crossed the hills near Shiraz and saw something which puzzled him. The hills of Shiraz were covered with old temples which had been cut into the rock of the mountainside. The ancient worshippers had disappeared centuries before and the temples were in a state of great decay. But clearly visible upon their walls, Barbaro noticed long legends written in a curious script which looked like a series of scratches made by a sharp nail.

When he returned he mentioned his discovery to his fellow-townsmen, but just then the Turks were threatening Europe with an invasion and people were too busy to bother about a new and unknown alphabet, somewhere in the heart of western Asia. The Persian inscriptions therefore were promptly forgotten.

Two and a half centuries later, a noble young Roman by the name of Pietro della Valle visited the same hillsides of Shiraz which Barbaro had passed two hundred years before. He, too, was puzzled by the strange inscriptions on the ruins and being a painstaking young fellow, he copied them carefully and sent his report together with some remarks about the trip to a friend of his, Doctor Schipano, who practiced medicine in Naples and who besides took an interest in matters of learning.

Schipano copied the funny little figures and brought them to the attention of other scientific men. Unfortunately Europe was again occupied with other matters.

The terrible wars between the Protestants and Catholics had broken out and people were busily killing those who disagreed with them upon certain points of a religious nature.

Another century was to pass before the study of the wedge-shaped inscriptions could be taken up seriously.

The eighteenth century—a delightful age for people of an active and curious mind—loved scientific puzzles. Therefore when King Frederick V of Denmark asked for men of learning to join an expedition which he was going to send to western Asia, he found no end of volunteers. His expedition, which left Copenhagen in 1761, lasted six years. During this period all of the members died except one, by the name of Karsten Niebuhr, who had begun life as a German peasant and could stand greater hardships than the professors who had spent their days amidst the stuffy books of their libraries.

This Niebuhr, who was a surveyor by profession, was a young man who deserves our admiration.

He continued his voyage all alone until he reached the ruins of Persepolis where he spent a month copying every inscription that was to be found upon the walls of the ruined palaces and temples.

After his return to Denmark he published his discoveries for the benefit of the scientific world and seriously tried to read some meaning into his own texts.

He was not successful.

But this does not astonish us when we understand the difficulties which he was obliged to solve.

When Champollion tackled the ancient Egyptian hieroglyphics he was able to make his studies from little pictures.

The writing of Persepolis did not show any pictures at all.

They consisted of V-shaped figures that were repeated endlessly and suggested nothing at all to the European eye.

Nowadays, when the puzzle has been solved we know that the original script of the Sumerians had been a picture-language, quite as much as that of the Egyptians.

But whereas the Egyptians at a very early date

had discovered the papyrus plant and had been able to paint their images upon a smooth surface, the inhabitants of Mesopotamia had been forced to carve their words into the hard rock of a mountain side or into a soft brick of clay.

Driven by necessity they had gradually simplified the original pictures until they devised a system of more than five hundred different letter-combinations which were necessary for their needs.

Let me give you a few examples. In the beginning, a star, when drawn with a nail into a brick looked as follows. ✳

But after a time the star shape was discarded as being too cumbersome and the figure was given this shape. ✳

After a while the meaning of "heaven" was added to that of "star," and the picture was simplified in this way ⊣ which made it still more of a puzzle.

In the same way an ox changed from ⋈ into ⊰ .

A fish changed from ⸙ into ⋇ . The sun, which was originally a plain circle, became ⊱ and if we were using the Sumerian script today we would make an ▰ look like this ⸰ᵃ .

You will understand how difficult it was to guess at the meaning of these figures but the patient labors of a German schoolmaster by the name of Grotefend was at last rewarded and thirty years after the first publication of Niebuhr's texts and three centuries after the first discovery of the wedge-formed pictures, four letters had been deciphered.

These four letters were the D, the A, the R and the Sh.

They formed the name of Darheush the King, whom we call Darius.

Then occurred one of those events which were only possible in those happy days before the telegraph-wire and the mail-steamer had turned the entire world into one large city.

While patient European professors were burning the midnight candles in their attempt to solve the new Asiatic mystery, young Henry Rawlinson was serving his time as a cadet of the British East Indian

Company.

He used his spare hours to learn Persian and when the Shah of Persia asked the English government for the loan of a few officers to train his native army, Rawlinson was ordered to go to Teheran. He travelled all over Persia and one day he happened to visit the village of Behistun. The Persians called it Bagistana which means the "dwellingplace of the Gods".

Centuries before the main road from Mesopotamia to Iran (the early home of the Persians) had run through this village and the Persian King Darius had used the steep walls of the high cliffs to tell all the world what a great man he was.

High above the roadside he had engraved an account of his glorious deeds.

The inscription had been made in the Persian language, in Babylonian and in the dialect of the city of Susa. To make the story plain to those who could not read at all, a fine piece of sculpture had been added showing the King of Persia placing his triumphant foot upon the body of Gaumata, the usurper who had tried to steal the throne away from the legitimate rulers. For good measure a dozen followers of Gaumata had been added. They stood in the background. Their hands were tied and they were to be executed in a few moments.

The picture and the three texts were several hundred feet above the road but Rawlinson scaled the walls of the rock at great danger to life and limb and copied the entire text.

His discovery was of the greatest importance. The Rock of Behistun became as famous as the Stone of Rosetta and Rawlinson shared the honors of deciphering the old nail-writing with Grotefend.

Although they had never seen each other or heard each other's names, the German schoolmaster and the British officer worked together for a common purpose as all good scientific men should do.

Their copies of the old text were reprinted in every land and by the middle of the nineteenth century, the cuneiform language (so called because the letters were wedge-shaped and "cuneus" is the Latin name for wedge) had given up its secrets. Another human mystery had been solved.

But about the people who had invented this clever way of writing, we have never been able to learn very much.

They were a white race and they were called the Sumerians.

They lived in a land which we call Shomer and which they themselves called Kengi, which means the "country of the reeds" and which shows us that they had dwelt among the marshy parts of the Mesopotamian valley. Originally the Sumerians had been mountaineers, but the fertile fields had tempted them away from the hills. But while they had left their ancient homes amidst the peaks of western Asia they had not given up their old habits and one of these is of particular interest to us.

Living amidst the peaks of western Asia, they had worshipped their Gods upon altars erected on the tops of rocks. In their new home, among the flat plains, there were no such rocks and it was impossible to construct their shrines in the old fashion. The Sumerians did not like this.

All Asiatic people have a deep respect for tradition and the Sumerian tradition demanded that an altar be plainly visible for miles around.

To overcome this difficulty and keep their peace with the Gods of their Fathers, the Sumerians had built a number of low towers (resembling little hills) on the top of which they had lighted their sacred fires in honor of the old divinities.

When the Jews visited the town of Bab-Illi (which we call Babylon) many centuries after the last of the Sumerians had died, they had been much impressed by the strange-looking towers which stood high amidst the green fields of Mesopotamia. The Tower of Babel of which we hear so much in the Old Testament was nothing but the ruin of an artificial peak, built hundreds of years before by a band of devout Sumerians. It was a curious contraption.

The Sumerians had not known how to construct

stairs.

They had surrounded their tower with a sloping gallery which slowly carried people from the bottom to the top.

A few years ago it was found necessary to build a new railroad station in the heart of New York City in such a way that thousands of travelers could be brought from the lower to the higher levels at the same moment.

It was not thought safe to use a staircase for in case of a rush or a panic people might have tumbled and that would have meant a terrible catastrophe.

To solve their problem the engineers borrowed an idea from the Sumerians.

And the Grand Central Station is provided with the same ascending galleries which had first been introduced into the plains of Mesopotamia, three thousand years ago.

十一　亚西利亚和巴比伦尼亚
——大塞姆的溶壶

　　我们常称美利坚为"溶壶"（Melting pot）。我们用这名词时，我们的意思是，有许多种族从地球的各部来聚居在沿大西洋和太平洋之滨，以寻一较在他们祖国所寻到的环境更相宜的新家而开始新的事业。这是真的，美索不达迷亚是较我们本国小的多。但是这肥泽的山谷是世所仅见的最非常的"溶壶"，它继续着吸收新的种族几乎有二千年。每族新的人民的在沿底格里斯和幼发拉的之滨夺取家宅的故事本是有趣味的，但是我只能给你们他们的企业之记录的很短的一节。

　　我们在前章所遇的萨谟利亚人刻划他们的历史于岩石和泥块上的（他们并非属于塞姆族），是漂泊进美索不达迷亚的第一群游牧。游牧是没有固定的家，五谷的田和菜蔬的园，只是住在篷帐之内，而看守他们的牛羊，而带了他们的牛羊和篷帐从这草原迁移到那草原的人民，他们在任何草绿水足的地方居住着。

广且远地他们的泥茅舍覆盖着平原。他们是善战者；他们能保存着他们的地位很久，抵抗一切的侵占者。

但是在四千年以前，有一族塞姆的沙漠之民叫作阿卡德人的离弃了阿剌伯，打败了萨谟利亚人而克取了美索不达迷亚。这些阿卡德人中最著名的王是叫萨尔恭。

他教他的百姓怎样用，那他们的领土才被他们占据去的萨谟利亚人的字母，来写他们自己的塞姆的言语。他是统治得如此聪明，就是原在者和侵入者之间的差异不久化为乌有了；他们成了密切的朋友而住在一起，安静而且谐和。

他的统辖的名声迅速地布满了西亚细亚和别的地方，听见了这成功的，被引来试试他们自己的运气。

有一沙漠之游牧的新族，叫亚摩利人的，解散了篷帐而向北进行。

那山谷是大纷扰的舞台，直至有一名叫罕默剌匹（或罕默剌比，随你的意）的亚摩利的酋长

罕默剌亚

自立于巴布伊利（这意思是上帝的门）城，而自做其大巴布伊利或巴比伦帝国的元首。

这罕默剌匹，他生在耶稣生前的二十一世纪，是一个很有兴味的人。他使得巴比伦成为古代的最重要的城，在那里有学问的教士，施行他们的大元首亲从太阳神收得的律法；在那里商人爱好行商，因为他是被待遇得公平而有礼貌。

真地若非为了地位的欠缺（这些罕默剌匹的律法会满占去如此的四十页，如其我将它们详细地写给你们），我可以指示你们：这古巴比伦国是较好几个近代的国家，在几方面治理得更好，人民是更愉快，法律与秩序维持得更谨慎，言论与思想更自由。

但是我们的世界永没有太完美的意思；不久别队狂暴而残忍的游牧从北方的山上下来，毁灭了这罕默剌匹的天才的工作。

这些新的侵占者的名字是喜泰人。关于这些

喜泰人我能告诉你们的，甚至比萨谟利亚人还要少。《圣经》提到他们。他们的文化的残迹已广且远地被寻到。他们用一种奇怪的象形文，但是还没有一个人能够阐明这些而读他们的意义。他们被赋做管理者的权并不厚，他们只管理了数年而他们的领土旋即一败堕地。

除了古怪的名字，和已经毁坏了许多别人用了不少的苦楚和困难建造起来的东西的名声以外，并没稍留关于一切的他们的荣誉。

于是来了别一个情形很是不同的侵袭。

有一族残酷的沙漠之漂泊者，他们用他们的大神亚苏之名屠杀而劫掠，离弃了阿剌伯而向北行进，直至他们到了山之斜坡。于是他们转向东，沿幼发拉的之滨，他们造了一座他们叫它做尼谑的城，这沿袭至今的名是一希腊文的尼尼微，立刻这些新来者，他们大概称做亚西利亚人，开始了一迟缓但是可惊的战争于一切的美索不达迷亚的别族居民。

在耶稣前的第十二世纪，他们第一次试欲毁灭巴比伦，但是他们的王提革拉毗色得到了这一次胜利后，他们便被击败不得不退到他们自己的国度去。

五百年后他们再试一次。一个名叫巴罗的勇猛将军，自做了亚西利亚王位之主。他假借了提革拉毗色，他是尊为亚西利亚人的国家的英雄的旧名，宣示了他的克服全世界的志愿。

他是言行如一。

小亚细亚，亚美尼亚，埃及，北阿剌伯，西波斯和巴比伦尼亚全成了亚西利亚的省份。它们被治于亚西利西的长官，他们征它们的税而强迫一切的少年在亚西利亚的军队中当兵；为了他们的贪得和残暴，他们自作的被一切的人憎恶而轻蔑着。

幸运地在它无上高位的亚西利亚帝国并没有持续得很久。这是像一只船有了太多的樯和帆而船身太小。那儿有了太多的兵士而农人不足——太多的将军而商人不足。

尼尼微

王和贵族日趋富足，但是庶民生活在污秽和贫困中。这国家从没有一刻是平和着的。它是永远为了种种缘故攻打或人，或处，这些缘故庶民是绝不顾及的。经了这不息而力竭的战争，直至大部的亚西利亚兵士已被杀死或残伤，这成了必须让外国人加入这军队。这些外国人不爱他们的那已毁坏了他们的家屋和已窃取了他们的儿女的残忍的主人，所以他们打的不好。

沿亚西利亚的疆界的生活不再安全。

外国的新族常在北面的边界袭击。其中之一叫作息米立亚人。息米立亚人，我们初次听到他们时，居住在北方之山外的广漠的平原上。荷马在他的奥德赛之行程的叙述中描写着他们的国家；他告诉我们这是一"永远浸在黑暗中"的地方。他们是白种人，他们也被另一群亚细亚的漂泊者，西徐亚人，驱出他们的老家。

西徐亚人是近代哥萨克人的祖先，甚至在那些遥远的日子，他们是著名于他们的骑马术的。

息米立亚人，受了西徐亚人的严酷的压迫的，从欧罗巴行进了亚细亚，克服了喜泰人的地方。于是他们离弃了小亚细亚的山头，而下降入美索不达迷亚的山谷中，在那里，他们于亚西利亚帝国之贫乏的人民中，作了可怖的蹂躏。

尼尼微，招志愿军以阻止这侵袭。当那更密接而可惊的危险的信息传来时，她的残败兵队便连忙向北进行。

有一小族叫作加尔底亚人的塞姆的游牧，平安地住在肥泽的山谷的东南部，叫作吾珥（Ur）国的里面。好几年突然地这些加尔底亚人走上了战道，开始了遭例的战役于亚西利亚人。

遭了各方面的袭击，这从未得到过一个邻人的好感的亚西利亚国是被宣告了死刑。

在尼尼微倾覆了，这被禁的，满贮以几世纪来的劫掠物的宝藏终究被毁灭了后，从波斯湾至尼罗河的每一茅舍和村落中都是欢乐。

在几代后希腊人游访幼发拉的，向这些生满了树枝的洪大的残迹是什么时候，没有一个人告诉他们。

人民已很快地忘了这城的真名，它曾有过一个如此残暴的主人而曾这般悲惨地虐待过他们的。

反之，巴比伦，它用相差很远的法子统治它的百姓的，复苏了。

当聪明的尼布甲尼撒王的久长的统辖时，古代的庙宇是重建着。广大的王宫是建筑在短期的时间内。全山谷掘满了新的运河以便灌溉田亩。好斗的邻人最严重地惩治着。

埃及是被征服做仅仅边疆的一省，耶路撒冷，犹太人的首都，是被毁灭了。摩西的《圣经》是被带到巴比伦而数千的犹太人是被迫的随了巴比伦王去他的首都，做那些留在巴力斯坦的人之公正的人质。

但是巴比伦是造成古代的七大奇观之一。

树是种在沿幼发拉的之滨。

花是植在许多的城墙上，数年后这似乎是从古城的顶上垂下了论千的花园。

加尔底亚人一造好他们的首都，世界的展览场，他们便集中他们的注意力于思想和精神的事务。

像一切的沙漠之民，他们深有兴趣于星，那在晚上引导他们安然经

尼尼微的倾覆

过了无迹的沙漠。

他们研究天象，他们提了天象的十二宫名。

他们作了天空的图表而发现了最初的五颗星球。他们提这些以他们的神祇的名字。罗马人克服了美索不达迷亚后，他们将加尔底亚的名字译成拉丁文；那解明为甚我们今日叫它们做朱匹忒（木星）、维纳索（金星）、马兹（火星）、麦邱立（水星）和萨腾（土星）。

他们分昼夜平分线为三百六十度，他们分昼夜为二十四小时，分时为六十分；于这老的巴比伦人的发明没有近代的人曾能改进过。他们没有表然而他们用日规的影计算时候。

他们知道兼用十进法和十二进法（如今我们只用十进法，那是很可怜的），十二进法（问你的父亲这字是什么意思）计数以六十分，六十秒和二十四小时，那似乎不大跟我们的近代世界相同，这当分昼夜为二十小时，分时为五十分和分分为

加尔底亚人

五十秒，照限定的十进法之例。

加尔底亚人也是承认有定期的休息日之必须的最早的人民。

他们分年为星期时，他们按排着六日的工作以后必得继续着一日献于"灵魂的安息"。

这是很可怜的，这如此富于勤勉和智慧的中心不能永远存在。但是，就是这辈最聪明的王们的天才，也不能保存这古代的美索不达迷亚的人民，于他们的最终的运命。

塞姆的世界是渐渐地老了。

这是给新族的人的时候了。

在耶稣前的第五世纪，有一族叫波斯人（关于他们等一下我要告诉你们）的印度欧罗巴人，离弃了伊兰的高山中的草原，克服了这肥泽的山谷。

巴比伦城是不战而得。

那伯尼特斯，末了的巴比伦王，他是更有趣味于宗教问题，较之那护卫他自己的国家，逃跑了。

几天后他的流落在后面的小儿子死了。

波斯王居鲁士十分敬重地葬了这小孩，就宣

布他是巴比伦尼亚的前元首的合法的继承者。

美索不达迷亚终了于做独立的国家了。

它成了波斯的一省给波斯的"巡抚"或知事统治着。

至于巴比伦，王们不再用这城做他们的居处时，它立刻失了一切的重要而仅仅成了一个乡村。

在耶稣前的第四世纪它再享受了片时的荣华。

这是在耶稣前的三百三十一年大亚历山大，刚征服了波斯，印度，埃及和其他的地方的希腊少年，访游这圣的忆念的古城。他要用这古城做他自己的新得的荣誉的背景。

他开始重建王宫而且命令扫除庙宇中的废物。

不幸地他很突然地死在尼布甲尼撒的宴饮殿中，自后地球上无物能保存巴比伦于她的残颓了。

一经亚历山大的将军之一的塞琉卡斯尼卡托完成了这在这大运河（这联合着底格里斯和幼发拉的）的口上做一新城的计划时，这巴比伦的命运便被断定了。

耶稣前的二百七十五年的一块碑告诉我们末了的巴比伦人怎样被逼的离别了他们的家乡，迁进这叫作塞琉细亚的新的居留地。

即在那时，也只几个有信心的人继续去拜访这圣地，那里现在是被狼和豺居住着。

大多数的人民，少有趣味于那些已往年代的半忘了的神祇；把它们的老家做成一更实际的应用品。

他们用它作石坑。

巴比伦是做了几乎三十世纪的塞姆世界的伟大的灵和智的中心；几百代的视它为人民的发挥他们天才最完备的城市。

它是古代的巴黎、伦敦和纽约。

此刻三个大的土坡指示我们，残墟已经隐埋在那有不息的侵占性的沙漠的沙土下面了。

XI. ASSYRIA AND BABYLONIA —THE GREAT SEMITIC MELTING POT

WE often call America the "Melting pot". When we use this term we mean that many races from all over the earth have gathered along the banks of the Atlantic and the Pacific Oceans to find a new home and begin a new career amidst more favorable surroundings than were to be found in the country of their birth. It is true, Mesopotamia was much smaller than our own country. But the fertile valley was the most extraordinary "melting pot" the world has ever seen and it continued to absorb new tribes for almost two thousand years. The story of each new people, clamoring for homesteads along the banks of the Tigris and the Euphrates is interesting in itself but we can give you only a very short record of their adventures.

The Sumerians whom we met in the previous chapter, scratching their history upon rocks and bits of clay (and who did not belong to the Semitic race) had been the first nomads to wander into Mesopotamia. Nomads are people who have no settled homes and no grain fields and no vegetable gardens but who live in tents and keep sheep and goats and cows and who move from pasture to pasture, taking their flocks and their tents wherever the grass is green and the water abundant.

Far and wide their mud huts had covered the plains. They were good fighters and for a long time they were able to hold their own against all invaders.

But four thousand years ago a tribe of Semitic desert people called the Akkadians left Arabia, defeated the Sumerians and conquered Mesopotamia. The most famous king of these Akkadians was called Sargon.

He taught his people how to write their own

Semitic language in the alphabet of the Sumerians whose territory they had just occupied. He ruled so wisely that soon the differences between the original settlers and the invaders disappeared and they became fast friends and lived together in peace and harmony.

The fame of his empire spread rapidly throughout western Asia and others, hearing of this success, they were tempted to try their own luck.

A new tribe of desert nomads, called the Amorites, broke up camp and moved northward.

Thereupon the valley was the scene of a great turmoil until an Amorite chieftain by the name of Hammurapi (or Hammurabi, as you please) established himself in the town of Bab-Illi (which means the Gate of the God) and made himself the ruler of a great Bab-Illian or Babylonian Empire.

This Hammurapi, who lived twenty-one centuries before the birth of Christ, was a very interesting man. He made Babylon the most important town of the ancient world, where learned priests administered the laws which their great Ruler had received from the Sun God himself and where the merchant loved to trade because he was treated fairly and honorably.

Indeed if it were not for the lack of space (these laws of Hammurapi would cover fully forty of these pages if I were to give them to you in detail) I would be able to show you that this ancient Babylonian State was in many respects better managed and that the people were happier and that law and order was maintained more carefully and that there was greater freedom of speech and thought than in many of our modern countries.

But our world was never meant to be too perfect and soon other hordes of rough and murderous men descended from the northern mountains and destroyed the work of Hammurapi's genius.

The name of these new invaders was the Hittites. Of these Hittites I can tell you even less than of the Sumerians. The Bible mentions them. Ruins of their civilization have been found far and wide. They used a strange sort of hieroglyphics but no one has as yet been able to decipher these and read their meaning. They were not greatly gifted as administrators. They ruled only a few years and then their domains fell to pieces.

Of all their glory there remains nothing but a mysterious name and the reputation of having destroyed many things which other people had built up with great pain and care.

Then came another invasion which was of a very different nature.

A fierce tribe of desert wanderers, who murdered and pillaged in the name of their great God Assur, left Arabia and marched northward until they reached the slopes of the mountains. Then they turned eastward and along the banks of the Euphrates they built a city which they called Ninua, a name which has come down to us in the Greek form of Nineveh. At once these new-comers, who are generally known as the Assyrians, began a slow but terrible warfare upon all the other inhabitants of Mesopotamia.

In the twelfth century before Christ they made

a first attempt to destroy Babylon but after a first success on the part of their King, Tiglath Pileser, they were defeated and forced to return to their own country.

Five hundred years later they tried again. An adventurous general by the name of Bulu made himself master of the Assyrian throne. He assumed the name of old Tiglath Pileser, who was considered the national hero of the Assyrians and announced his intention of conquering the whole world.

He was as good as his word.

Asia Minor and Armenia and Egypt and Northern Arabia and Western Persia and Babylonia became Assyrian provinces. They were ruled by Assyrian governors, who collected the taxes and forced all the young men to serve as soldiers in the Assyrian armies and who made themselves thoroughly hated and despised both for their greed and their cruelty.

Fortunately the Assyrian Empire at its greatest height did not last very long. It was like a ship with too many masts and sails and too small a hull. There were too many soldiers and not enough farmers—too many generals and not enough business men.

The King and the nobles grew very rich but the masses lived in squalor and poverty. Never for a moment was the country at peace. It was for ever fighting someone, somewhere, for causes which did not interest the subjects at all. Until, through this continuous and exhausting warfare, most of the Assyrian soldiers had been killed or maimed and it became necessary to allow foreigners to enter the army. These foreigners had little love for their brutal masters who had destroyed their homes and had stolen their children and therefore they fought badly.

Life along the Assyrian frontier was no longer safe.

Strange new tribes were constantly attacking the northern boundaries. One of these was called the Cimmerians. The Cimmerians, when we first hear of them, inhabited the vast plain beyond the northern mountains. Homer describes their country in his account of the voyage of Odysseus and he tells us that it was a place "for ever steeped in darkness". They were a race of white men and they had been driven out of their former homes by still another group of Asiatic wanderers, the Scythians.

The Scythians were the ancestors of the modern Cossacks, and even in those remote days they were famous for their horsemanship.

The Cimmerians, hard pressed by the Scythians, crossed from Europe into Asia and conquered the land of the Hittites. Then they left the mountains of Asia Minor and descended into the valley of Mesopotamia, where they wrought terrible havoc among the impoverished people of the Assyrian Empire.

Nineveh called for volunteers to stop this invasion. Her worn-out regiments marched northward when news came of a more immediate and formidable danger.

For many years a small tribe of Semitic nomads, called the Chaldeans, had been living peacefully in the south-eastern part of the fertile valley, in the country called Ur. Suddenly these Chaldeans had gone upon the war-path and had begun a regular campaign against the Assyrians.

Attacked from all sides, the Assyrian State, which had never gained the good-will of a single neighbor, was doomed to perish.

When Nineveh fell and this forbidding treasure house, filled with the plunder of centuries, was at last destroyed, there was joy in every hut and hamlet from the Persian Gulf to the Nile.

And when the Greeks visited the Euphrates a few generations later and asked what these vast ruins, covered with shrubs and trees might be, there was no one to tell them.

The people had hastened to forget the very name of the city that had been such a cruel master and had so miserably oppressed them.

Babylon, on the other hand, which had ruled its subjects in a very different way, came back to life.

During the long reign of the wise King Nebuchadnezzar the ancient temples were rebuilt. Vast palaces were erected within a short space of time. New canals were dug all over the valley to help irrigate the fields. Quarrelsome neighbors were severely punished.

Egypt was reduced to a mere frontier-province and Jerusalem, the capital of the Jews, was destroyed. The Holy Books of Moses were taken to Babylon and several thousand Jews were forced to follow the Babylonian King to his capital as hostages for the good behavior of those who remained behind in Palestine.

But Babylon was made into one of the seven wonders of the ancient world.

Trees were planted along the banks of the Euphrates.

Flowers were made to grow upon the many walls of the city and after a few years it seemed that a thousand gardens were hanging from the roofs of the ancient town.

As soon as the Chaldeans had made their capital the show-place of the world they devoted their attention to matters of the mind and of the spirit.

Like all desert folk they were deeply interested

in the stars which at night had guided them safely through the trackless desert.

They studied the heavens and named the twelve signs of the Zodiac.

They made maps of the sky and they discovered the first five planets. To these they gave the names of their Gods. When the Romans conquered Mesopotamia they translated the Chaldean names into Latin and that explains why today we talk of Jupiter and Venus and Mars and Mercury and Saturn.

They divided the equator into three hundred and sixty degrees and they divided the day into twenty-four hours and the hour into sixty minutes and no modern man has ever been able to improve upon this old Babylonian invention. They possessed no watches but they measured time by the shadow of the sun-dial.

They learned to use both the decimal and the duodecimal systems (nowadays we use only the decimal system, which is a great pity). The duodecimal system (ask your father what the word means), accounts for the sixty minutes and the sixty seconds and the twenty-four hours which seem to have so little in common with our modern world which would have divided day and night into twenty hours and the hour into fifty minutes and the minute into fifty seconds according to the rules of the restricted decimal system.

The Chaldeans also were the first people to recognize the necessity of a regular day of rest.

When they divided the year into weeks they ordered that six days of labor should be followed by one day, devoted to the "peace of the soul".

It was a great pity that the center of so much intelligence and industry could not exist for ever. But not even the genius of a number of very wise Kings could save the ancient people of Mesopotamia from their ultimate fate.

The Semitic world was growing old.

It was time for a new race of men.

In the fifth century before Christ, an Indo-European people called the Persians (I shall tell you about them later) left its pastures amidst the high mountains of Iran and conquered the fertile valley.

The city of Babylon was captured without a struggle.

Nabonidus, the last Babylonian king, who had been more interested in religious problems than in defending his own country, fled.

A few days later his small son, who had remained behind, died.

Cyrus, the Persian King, buried the child with great honor and then proclaimed himself the legitimate successor of the old rulers of Babylonia.

Mesopotamia ceased to be an independent State.

It became a Persian province ruled by a Persian "Satrap" or Governor.

As for Babylon, when the Kings no longer used the city as their residence it soon lost all importance and became a mere country village.

In the fourth century before Christ it enjoyed another spell of glory.

It was in the year 331 B.C. that Alexander the

Great, the young Greek who had just conquered
Persia and India and Egypt and every other place,
visited the ancient city of sacred memories. He
wanted to use the old city as a background for his
own newly-acquired glory. He began to rebuild the
palace and ordered that the rubbish be removed from
the temples.

Unfortunately he died quite suddenly in the
Banqueting Hall of Nebuchadnezzar and after that
nothing on earth could save Babylon from her ruin.

As soon as one of Alexander's generals, Seleucus
Nicator, had perfected the plans for a new city at the
mouth of the great canal which united the Tigris and
the Euphrates, the fate of Babylon was sealed.

A tablet of the year 275 B.C. tells us how the last
of the Babylonians were forced to leave their home
and move into this new settlement which had been
called Seleucia.

Even then, a few of the faithful continued to visit
the holy places which were now inhabited by wolves
and jackals.

The majority of the people, little interested in those half-forgotten divinities of a bygone age, made a more practical use of their former home.

They used it as a stone-quarry.

For almost thirty centuries Babylon had been the great spiritual and intellectual center of the Semitic world and a hundred generations had regarded the city as the most perfect expression of their people's genius.

It was the Paris and London and New York of the ancient world.

At present three large mounds show us where the ruins lie buried beneath the sand of the ever-encroaching desert.

十二　摩西的故事

在远远一条细细的地平线上面的空中，显现着一小块尘沙。巴比伦的农人在这肥沃之地的边境上，正耕着他的瘦瘠的田亩，忽然注意到了它。

"又是一族要想侵入我们的国境，"他对他自己说，"他们不会去得远的，王的兵士会驱开他们。"

他是对的。边疆的护卫兵拔刀出鞘，向着新到者，请他们去别处寻他们的机会。

他们随了巴比伦的边界向西进行，他们漂泊着直至他们到了地中海之滨。

在那里，他们住下了，看守他们的羊群，过着他们最初的祖先（他们曾住在乌拉山）的简单的生活。

后来这个地方终年不雨，食物不足，人和动物都受恐慌。如果不另外寻找新的草原，就要饿死在这个地方了。

这群牧羊人（他们是叫作希伯来人）再迁他们的家室进一新的去处，这是他们在近埃及地方的沿红海之滨寻得的。

但是饥饿和缺乏又追随在他们的行程后面；他们又不得不到埃及的官员处去哀哀乞怜，苟延残喘。

埃及人早预期着荒年，他们已造了大的贮藏室，这些贮藏室中全满贮了七年来的盈余的麦。现在麦是在人群中分派着，一个粮食官受了任命，将它均量地分派给富者和贫者，他的名字是约瑟，他是属于希伯来族。

他还是在当小孩子的时候，从他自己的家庭里逃出来的。据说他的逃走是为了保全他自己，免得触怒了他的兄弟们——他们之所以嫉忌约瑟，就因为他们的父亲顶爱约瑟，不爱他们。

这是真实的，约瑟去了埃及，得到了喜克索王的眷顾；喜克索王刚征服了这国家，任用了这英俊的少年，以辅助他们管理他们的新的所有物。

饥饿的希伯来人刚显现在约瑟前求助时，约

瑟便认出了他的亲戚。

但是他是宽宏的人，一切卑鄙的念头，对于他的灵魂是疏远的。

他对于那些曾经谋害过他的人，不念旧恶。他反而给他们许多麦，让他们住在埃及——他们，他们的儿女和他们的羊群全过着快适的生活。

希伯来人（他们是更普通地称做犹太人）是住在他们的承继国的东部好多年，一切与他们无忤。

接着发生了一桩大的变化。

一个突然的变革夺去了喜克索王的政权，逼他们离开了这国度，埃及人又是他们本族中的主人了。他们再也不善遇外国人了。受了一辈阿剌伯的牧羊人的三百年的压迫，增大了这憎恶一切凡是外国东西的情感。

在别方面，犹太人跟喜克索人是亲密的，他们和他们有血统和种族上的关系，这在埃及人的目中看来，是足够证明他们是反叛者了。

约瑟不再住着以保护他的同胞。

在一短的挣扎后，他们是被移出他们的老

家，被逐进这国度的中心而被待遇如奴隶。

他们是做了许多年普通工人乏味的工作，搬运石头以建金字塔，为公共的大厦制砖瓦，建筑街道。并掘运河，使尼罗河的水流到远隔着的埃及人的田亩。

他们受的痛苦是重的，但是他们始终没有失去毅力。现在救星快要到了。

那儿住着某少年，他的名字是摩西。他是很智慧的，而且他受了好的教育，因为埃及人已定当了他要去服务法老。

如其没有挑他的愤怒的事情发生，摩西会平静地毕生做着一小省的知事或是外县的征税官。

但是埃及人，如我已在前对你们说过的，轻蔑着那些相貌不跟他们自己一样，衣服也不照真的埃及人的式样的人，而且他们还时常侮辱这种人，因为他们是"不同的"。

而且因为外国人是占少数，他们不能善护他们自己。这也并没任何的成效，以呈他们的控诉于公庭前，因为裁判官并不同情于一个拒绝着崇拜埃及的神，和用着浓郁的外国的音调申诉他的案情的人的冤屈。

现在发生了一件事，一日摩西跟几个他的埃及朋友在散步，其中之一说了些特别干犯犹太人的话，甚至于恫吓着说是要捉他们。

摩西是一烈性的少年，打了他一拳头。

这一拳头太厉害了些，竟把那个埃及人打死了。杀死一个本国人是可惊的事，而且埃及人的法律是没有善良的巴比伦王罕默剌匹的那些公正——巴比伦王承认存心谋杀，与受了侮辱迫而杀人是不同的。在埃及人看了不管你动机怎么样，只要是杀人，就不是好东西。

摩西逃走了。

他逃进了他的祖先的地方，逃进了米甸的沙漠沿红海的东岸，在几百年的以前他的一族曾在那里看守过他们的羊群。

一个名叫叶忒罗的仁爱的教士，收留了他在家里，将自己七个女儿中之一的西坡拉给他做妻子。

摩西在那里住了很久，他在那里沉思着许多深奥的问题。他已离别了法老的奢华而安适的王宫，来分享这沙漠的教士的粗糙而单调的生活。

昔日在犹太人已迁入埃及以前，他们也是阿

剌伯的无穷的平原中的漂泊者。他们住在篷帐内，吃平凡的食物，但是他们的男子是笃实的，女子是忠诚的，物质的欲望很小，只是骄傲着他们的心灵的至善。

在他们已沐浴着埃及的文化后，一切全改变了。他们已学了爱好欢乐的埃及人的样子。他们让别一族人统治着他们，而他们无意于为他们的独立战争。

替代了旋风的沙漠的旧神，他们开始崇拜着住在黑暗的埃及庙宇里光耀的奇怪的神祇。

摩西觉得这是他的责职，前去从他们的灭亡保全他的同胞，而领他们回到昔日的单纯的信仰。

所以他遣了一个送信人到他的亲属处去，对他们提议。他们离弃了这个做奴隶的地方，跟随他到沙漠去。

但是埃及人听到了这信息，较前更留意地看守着犹太人。

这似乎是摩西的方略命中注定应该失败的，尼罗河流域的人民中突然发现了一种传染病。

那常遵守着某种很精确的卫生律（这是他们在他们沙漠生活的艰苦日子中学得的）的犹太

人避免了这种病，而软弱的埃及人是几百千的死着。

摩西

在随着这"寂寞之死"而来的纷乱和惊慌中，犹太人包扎了他们的一切物件，赶速从那应许他们如此之多而赠与他们这般的少的地方逃出去。

这逃跑一经发觉，埃及人马上想用他们的军队追赶他们，但是他们的兵士遇到了灾祸，而犹太人逃走了。

他们是平安的，他们是自由的，他们向东迁入了荒凉的空地，这是位于赛奈峰之麓——这峰的名字是从巴比伦的月亮神辛起的。

在那里，摩西指挥着他的同族人，开始他的伟大的改革的工作。

犹太人像一切的别的人民，在那些日子是崇拜多神的。当他们住在埃及时，他们曾学得了崇奉那些动物为神，对于这些，埃及人是抑制着如此崇高的敬礼，他们造了圣的神龛，为了他们的特殊的利益。反之，摩西当他的久长而寂寞的生活于半岛的沙山中，学得了崇敬这伟大的风雨雷电之神的强力，他是管理着高高的上天，沙漠中的漂泊者把他们的生命，光和呼吸依靠着他的仁慈。

这神是叫耶和华，他是一个有权力的生物，他是被西亚细亚的塞姆的一切的人民低首地小心翼翼地崇敬着。

经了摩西的教导，他是成了犹太族的唯一之主。

一日摩西从希伯来人的篷帐不见了。他随身带着两块粗刻了的石碑。这是耳语着，他去赛奈峰的最高点去寻求隐居了。

那天下午，山的顶是看不见了。

一个可惊的风潮的黑暗，从人的眼睛隐藏了它。

但是摩西回转来时，看啊！……那儿站着两块刻着耶和华亲自在他的雷的轰轰声和电的炫目的闪光中所讲的话的碑。

从那时以后，没有一个犹太人再敢怀疑摩西的威权了。

他告诉他的同胞，耶和华命令他们继续着他们的漂泊，他们热诚地服从着。

他们住在沙漠的无迹的山中许多年。

他们遭受着非常的艰辛，几乎灭亡于食物和水的缺乏。

但是摩西崇高地实践了他们的"应许地"的希望，它会把一个真的家供给耶和华的真实的跟从者。

终究他们达到了一个更肥沃的境界。

他们经过了约旦河，他们带了"律法的圣碑"，预备占据这从澹展至别是巴的草原。

至于摩西，他不再是他们的领袖了。

他已渐渐地老起来，他很是疲惫。

他已被许可着看看远离的巴力斯坦山的山脊，从中犹太人找到了一个祖国。

于是他永远地闭着他的智慧的眼睛。

他已完成了在他少年时开始的工作。

他已领导了他的同胞从外国奴而到了独立生存的新自由。

他已团结了他们，使他们成了一切崇拜唯一的上帝的第一国。

XII. THIS IS THE STORY OF MOSES

HIGH above the thin line of the distant horizon there appeared a small cloud of dust. The Babylonian peasant, working his poor farm on the outskirts of the fertile lands, noticed it.

"Another tribe is trying to break into our land," he said to himself. "They will not get far. The King's soldiers will drive them away."

He was right. The frontier guards welcomed the new arrivals with drawn swords and bade them try their luck elsewhere.

They moved westward following the borders of the land of Babylon and they wandered until they reached the shores of the Mediterranean.

There they settled down and tended their flocks and lived the simple lives of their earliest ancestors who had dwelt in the land of Ur.

Then there came a time when the rain ceased to fall and there was not enough to eat for man or beast and it became necessary to look for new pastures or perish on the spot.

Once more the shepherds (who were called the Hebrews) moved their families into a new home which they found along the banks of the Red Sea near the land of Egypt.

But hunger and want had followed them upon their voyage and they were forced to go to the Egyptian officials and beg for food that they might not starve.

The Egyptians had long expected a famine. They had built large store-houses and these were all filled with the surplus wheat of the last seven years. This wheat was now being distributed among the people and a food-dictator had been appointed to deal it out equally to the rich and to the poor. His name was Joseph and he belonged to the tribe of the Hebrews.

As a mere boy he had run away from his own

family. It was said that he had escaped to save himself from the anger of his brethren who envied him because he was the favorite of their Father.

Whatever the truth, Joseph had gone to Egypt and he had found favor in the eyes of the Hyksos Kings who had just conquered the country and who used this bright young man to assist them in administering their new possessions.

As soon as the hungry Hebrews appeared before Joseph with their request for help, Joseph recognized his relatives.

But he was a generous man and all meanness of spirit was foreign to his soul.

He did not revenge himself upon those who had wronged him but he gave them wheat and allowed them to settle in the land of Egypt, they and their children and their flocks—and be happy.

For many years the Hebrews (who are more commonly known as the Jews) lived in the eastern part of their adopted country and all was well with them.

Then a great change took place.

A sudden revolution deprived the Hyksos Kings of their power and forced them to leave the country. Once more the Egyptians were masters within their own house. They had never liked foreigners any too well. Three hundred years of oppression by a band of Arab shepherds had greatly increased this feeling of loathing for everything that was alien.

The Jews on the other hand had been on friendly terms with the Hyksos who were related to them by blood and by race. This was enough to make them traitors in the eyes of the Egyptians.

Joseph no longer lived to protect his people.

After a short struggle they were taken away from their old homes, they were driven into the heart of the country and they were treated like slaves.

For many years they performed the dreary tasks of common laborers, carrying stones for the building of pyramids, making bricks for public buildings, constructing roads, and digging canals to carry the water of the Nile to the distant Egyptian farms.

Their suffering was great but they never lost courage and help was near.

There lived a certain young man whose name was Moses. He was very intelligent and he had received a good education because the Egyptians had decided that he should enter the service of Pharaoh.

If nothing had happened to arouse his anger, Moses would have ended his days peacefully as the governor of a small province or the collector of taxes of an outlying district.

But the Egyptians, as I have told you before, despised those who did not look like themselves nor dress in true Egyptian fashion and they were apt to insult such people because they were "different".

And because the foreigners were in the minority they could not well defend themselves. Nor did it serve any good purpose to carry their complaints before a tribunal for the Judge did not smile upon the grievances of a man who refused to worship the Egyptian gods and who pleaded his case with a strong foreign accent.

Now it occurred one day that Moses was taking a walk with a few of his Egyptian friends and one of these said something particularly disagreeable about the Jews and even threatened to lay hands on them.

Moses, who was a hot-headed youth hit him.

The blow was a bit too severe and the Egyptian fell down dead.

To kill a native was a terrible thing and the Egyptian laws were not as wise as those of Hammurapi, the good Babylonian King, who recognized the difference between a premeditated murder and the killing of a man whose insults had brought his opponent to a point of unreasoning rage.

Moses fled.

He escaped into the land of his ancestors, into the Midian desert, along the eastern bank of the Red Sea, where his tribe had tended their sheep several hundred years before.

A kind priest by the name of Jethro received him in his house and gave him one of his seven daughters, Zipporah, as his wife.

There Moses lived for a long time and there he pondered upon many deep subjects. He had left the luxury and the comfort of the palace of Pharaoh to share the rough and simple life of a desert priest.

In the olden days, before the Jewish people had moved into Egypt, they too had been wanderers among the endless plains of Arabia. They had lived in tents and they had eaten plain food, but they had been honest men and faithful women, contented with few possessions but proud of the righteousness of their mind.

All this had been changed after they had become exposed to the civilization of Egypt. They had taken to the ways of the comfort-loving Egyptians. They had allowed another race to rule them and they had not cared to fight for their independence.

Instead of the old gods of the wind-swept desert they had begun to worship strange divinities who lived in the glimmering splendors of the dark Egyptian temples.

Moses felt that it was his duty to go forth and save

his people from their fate and bring them back to the simple Truth of the olden days.

And so he sent messengers to his relatives and suggested that they leave the land of slavery and join him in the desert.

But the Egyptians heard of this and guarded the Jews more carefully than ever before.

It seemed that the plans of Moses were doomed to failure when suddenly an epidemic broke out among the people of the Nile Valley.

The Jews who had always obeyed certain very strict laws of health (which they had learned in the hardy days of their desert life) escaped the disease while the weaker Egyptians died by the hundreds of thousands.

Amidst the confusion and the panic which followed this Silent Death, the Jews packed their belongings and hastily fled from the land which had promised them so much and which had given them so little.

As soon as the flight became known the Egyptians

tried to follow them with their armies but their soldiers met with disaster and the Jews escaped.

They were safe and they were free and they moved eastward into the waste spaces which are situated at the foot of Mount Sinai, the peak which has been called after Sin, the Babylonian God of the Moon.

There Moses took command of his fellow-tribesmen and commenced upon his great task of reform.

In those days, the Jews, like all other people, worshipped many gods. During their stay in Egypt they had even learned to do homage to those animals which the Egyptians held in such high honor that they built holy shrines for their special benefit. Moses on the other hand, during his long and lonely life amidst the sandy hills of the peninsula, had learned to revere the strength and the power of the great God of the Storm and the Thunder, who ruled the high heavens and upon whose good-will the wanderer in the desert depended for life and light and breath.

This God was called Jehovah and he was a mighty Being who was held in trembling respect by all the Semitic people of western Asia.

Through the teaching of Moses he was to become the sole Master of the Jewish race.

One day Moses disappeared from the camp of the Hebrews. He took with him two tablets of rough-hewn stone. It was whispered that he had gone to seek the solitude of Mount Sinai's highest peak.

That afternoon, the top of the mountain was lost to sight.

The darkness of a terrible storm hid it from the eye of man.

But when Moses returned, behold! ... There stood engraved upon the tablets the words which Jehovah himself had spoken amidst the crash of his thunder and the blinding flashes of his lightning.

From that moment on, no Jew dared to question the authority of Moses.

When he told his people that Jehovah commanded

them to continue their wanderings, they obeyed with eagerness.

For many years they lived amidst the trackless hills of the desert.

They suffered great hardships and almost perished from lack of food and water.

But Moses kept high their hopes of a Promised Land which would offer a lasting home to the true followers of Jehovah.

At last they reached a more fertile region.

They crossed the river Jordan and, carrying the Holy Tablets of Law, they made ready to occupy the pastures which stretch from Dan to Beersheba.

As for Moses, he was no longer their leader.

He had grown old and he was very tired.

He had been allowed to see the distant ridges of the Palestine Mountains among which the Jews were to find a Fatherland.

Then he had closed his wise eyes for all time.

He had accomplished the task which he had set himself in his youth.

He had led his people out of foreign slavery into the new freedom of an independent life.

He had united them and he had made them the first of all nations to worship a single God.

十三　耶路撒冷——律法的城市

巴力斯坦是一小带地方，位于叙利亚的山和地中海的绿水之间。它自从不可追忆的时候起，就被人民居住着，我们对于最初居留的人民，虽然已给他们起了一个迦南人的名称，其实对于他们是不大十分了解的。

迦南人是寓于塞姆族。他们的祖先，像那些犹太人和巴比伦人一样，是沙漠之民，但是犹太人进巴力斯坦时，迦南人是住在城镇和村庄中了。他们不再是牧羊人而是商人了。真的，在犹太的言语中，迦南人和商人是同一意义的。

他们已亲自造了坚固的城市，环绕着高的城墙，不许犹太人进他们的城门，但是他们逼得他们固守在旷野，而建他们的家于山谷的草地中。

虽然，隔了没有多时，犹太人和迦南人成了朋友。这并不很困难，因为他们俩是属于同一族的。再则，他们惧怕一个共同的仇敌，只有他们的联合着的坚力，能防御他们的国家于这些危险的邻人，他们是叫作非利士人而且他们是完全地属于异族。

确然的，非利士人是不应在亚细亚的。他们是欧罗巴人，他们的最早的家是在克里特岛中。在什么时代他们已散居在沿地中海之滨不十分确定，因为我们不知道在什么时代印度欧罗巴的侵占者已从他们的岛的家驱逐了他们。但是甚至埃及人，他们叫他们做普剌萨底，也很怕他们，当非利士人（他们戴一羽毛的头巾，正如我们的印第安人）走上战道时，西亚细亚的一切的人民全遭了大军去保护他们的边疆。

至于非利士人和犹太人之间的战争，它从没得到了结束。因为虽然大卫杀了歌利亚（他穿一套在那些日子看来是大神奇的铠甲，这无疑地是从塞浦路斯岛输入的，在那儿寻得了古代的铜矿），虽然参孙杀了非利士人，当他葬他自己和他的仇敌于对衮庙的下面时，非利士人还是常自认优胜于犹太人，终不许希伯来人得握任何地中海的海口。

因此犹太人是被命运所逼的知足着他们的东

耶路撒冷

巴力斯坦的山谷，而他们在那里的不毛之山的顶上建立着他们的首都。

这城的名字是耶路撒冷，它是做了三千年的西方世界的最圣的地方之一。

在不可知的过去的蒙昧时代，耶路撒冷，"和平之家"，是埃及人的一小座巩固的前哨，埃及人在沿巴力斯坦的山脉建了许多小的堡垒和城寨，以防御他们的远隔的疆界对于从东方来的袭击。

埃及帝国倾覆了后，有一土族泽部息人迁进了这被弃的城市。继而犹太人在一久长的竞争后，占据了这城，使它做了他们的大卫王的居处。

终究，在许多年的漂泊后，这个"律法碑"似乎达到了一个久息的场所。智者的所罗门定当了供给它们以一庄严的寓所。他的使者到处去为珍奇的木材和贵重的金属遍搜这世界。全国是被请着供奉它的富源以使这"上帝之家"卓越于它的圣名。逐渐逐渐地这庙宇的墙高起来，永久护卫着这圣的耶和华的法律。

唉，期待着的，永久是证明了不能持久。在敌视的邻人中的侵占者的他们自己，各方面给仇敌包围着，给非利士人扰累着，犹太人并不维持他们的独立很久。

他们打的尽善而勇敢。但是他们的小小的国家，致弱于细小的妒忌，是轻易地给亚西利亚人，埃及人和加尔底亚人克服着；当巴比伦王，尼布甲尼撒在耶稣生前五百八十六年得到了耶路撒冷，他毁坏了这城和殿，而石碑于大火中升了起来。

立刻，犹太人动工重造他们的圣殿。但是所罗门的荣华的日子是过去了。犹太人是外族的百姓，金钱又不多。经过了七十年，重造起这如前的大厦。圣殿平安地存立了三百年，但是接着又发生了第二次的侵袭，燃烧着的殿的红焰又照耀在巴力斯坦的天空中了。

当圣殿第三次重造着时，四围包着两座高的城墙，开着狭的门，并加上了几条不能通行的里巷，以防御将来突然的侵袭。

但是不幸追逐着耶路撒冷城。

在耶稣生前的第六十五年，在他们的庞培将军下的罗马人占有了犹太人的首都。他们的实际主义并不表同情于一个有弯曲而黑暗的街道，和许多不卫生的小巷的古旧的城市。他们打扫了这旧废物（他们是这样想的）而造了新的营盘，大的公共建筑物、游泳池和体育场；他们强迫着不愿意出钱的庶民纳税，使得市政改良。

那座没有实际用处的殿他们早就见到是被忽略着，直至赫洛德（Herod）的日子，他是给罗马的刀所任命的犹太人的王，他的自负是盼望更新这已往时代的古昔的荣耀。在冷淡的状态中，被压迫着的人民着手服从那非他们亲选的主人的命令。

当末了的一块石头已被置于它的准确的所在时，又一对于不仁的罗马的征税官的革命发生了。这殿是这次暴动的第一件牺牲品。泰塔斯皇帝的兵士迅速地放火，焚烧这古犹太人之信仰的中心点。不过耶路撒冷城还不曾遭殃。

然而巴力斯坦继续做了不安的舞台。

那熟悉各种的人类，并管理着崇拜成千种不

同的神祇的国家的罗马人，并不知道怎样处置犹太人。他们一些不明白犹太人的性格。绝端的容忍（由于冷淡）是罗马创立她的很成功的帝国的基础。罗马的长官从不干预属民的宗教信仰。他们所需要的是住在罗马领土的远离的部分的人民的庙中，置一皇帝的图像或雕像。这不过是一惯例，并没什么深奥的寓意。但是对于犹太人，如此的事情似乎是很渎神的，他们不愿来雕刻一个罗马皇帝的像，亵渎他们的众圣之圣。

他们拒绝着。

罗马人坚持着。

本来是件不大重要的事，这类的不了解是继续增长而使得恶感更深。在泰培斯皇帝下的背叛后五十二年，犹太人又反抗了。这次罗马人决定了贯彻他们的破坏的工作。

耶路撒冷是被毁灭了。

这殿是被烧尽了。

在所罗门的古城的残墟上，建造着一座叫作伊立亚卡匹托立那的新的罗马城。

一个奉献于崇拜周比特的异教徒的庙，是建造在那笃信的人已崇拜了耶和华几乎一千年的原址上。

住在首都的犹太人全被罗马人驱逐出去，还有几千人是从他们的祖先的家乡被罗马人驱散。

从那时起，他们成了地球上的漂泊者。

但是圣的律法不再需要尊严殿宇的庇护了。

《圣经》中的律法已经广播，不限于犹太一隅之地。《圣经》成了公正生活的象征，凡是高尚的人，要想过着正当生活，是不能不读它的。

XIII. JERUSALEM
—THE CITY OF THE LAW

PALESTINE is a small strip of land between the mountains of Syria and the green waters of the Mediterranean. It has been inhabited since time immemorial, but we do not know very much about the first settlers, although we have given them the name of Canaanites.

The Canaanites belonged to the Semitic race. Their ancestors, like those of the Jews and the Babylonians, had been a desert folk. But when the Jews entered Palestine, the Canaanites lived in towns and villages. They were no longer shepherds but traders. Indeed, in the Jewish language, Canaanite and merchant came to mean the same thing.

They had built themselves strong cities, surrounded by high walls and they did not allow the Jews to enter their gates, but they forced them to keep to the open country and make their home amidst the grassy lands of the valleys.

After a time, however, the Jews and the Canaanites became friends. This was not so very difficult for they both belonged to the same race. Besides they feared a common enemy and only their united strength could defend their country against these dangerous neighbors, who were called the Philistines and who belonged to an entirely different race.

The Philistines really had no business in Asia. They were Europeans, and their earliest home had been in the Isle of Crete. At what age they had settled along the shores of the Mediterranean is quite uncertain because we do not know when the Indo-European invaders had driven them from their island home. But even the Egyptians, who called them Purasati, had feared them greatly and when the Philistines (who wore a headdress of feathers just like our Indians) went upon the war-path, all the people of western Asia sent large armies to protect their frontiers.

As for the war between the Philistines and the Jews, it never came to an end. For although David slew Goliath (who wore a suit of armor which was a great curiosity in those days and had been no doubt imported from the island of Cyprus where the copper mines of the ancient world were found) and although Samson killed the Philistines wholesale when he buried himself and his enemies beneath the temple of Dagon, the Philistines always proved themselves more than a match for the Jews and never allowed the Hebrew people to get hold of any of the harbors of the Mediterranean.

The Jews therefore were obliged by fate to content themselves with the valleys of eastern Palestine and there, on the top of a barren hill, they erected their capital.

The name of this city was Jerusalem and for thirty centuries it has been one of the most holy spots of the western world.

In the dim ages of the unknown past, Jerusalem, the Home of Peace, had been a little fortified outpost of the Egyptians who had built many small fortifications and castles along the mountain ridges of Palestine, to defend their outlying frontier against attacks from the East.

After the downfall of the Egyptian Empire, a native tribe, the Jebusites, had moved into the deserted city. Then came the Jews who captured the town after a long struggle and made it the residence of their King David.

At last, after many years of wandering the Tables of the Law seemed to have reached a place of enduring rest. Solomon, the Wise, decided to provide them with a magnificent home. Far and wide his messengers travelled to ransack the world for rare woods and precious metals. The entire nation was asked to offer its wealth to make the House of God worthy of its holy name. Higher and higher the walls of the temple arose guarding the sacred Laws of Jehovah for all the ages.

Alas, the expected eternity proved to be of short duration. Themselves intruders among hostile neighbors, surrounded by enemies on all sides, harassed by the Philistines, the Jews did not maintain their independence for very long.

They fought well and bravely. But their little state, weakened by petty jealousies, was easily overpowered by the Assyrians and the Egyptians and the Chaldeans and when Nebuchadnezzar, the King of Babylon, took Jerusalem in the year 586 before the birth of Christ, he destroyed the city and the temple, and the Tablets of Stone went up in the general conflagration.

At once the Jews set to work to rebuild their holy shrine. But the days of Solomon's glory were gone. The Jews were the subjects of a foreign race and money was scarce. It took seventy years to reconstruct the old edifice. It stood securely for three hundred years but then a second invasion took place and once more the red flames of the burning temple brightened the skies of Palestine.

When it was rebuilt for the third time, it was surrounded by two high walls with narrow gates and several inner courts were added to make sudden invasion in the future an impossibility.

But ill-luck pursued the city of Jerusalem.

In the sixty-fifth year before the birth of Christ, the Romans under their general Pompey took possession of the Jewish capital. Their practical sense did not take kindly to an old city with crooked and dark streets and many unhealthy alley-ways. They cleaned up this old rubbish (as they considered it) and built new barracks and large public buildings and swimming-pools and athletic parks and they forced their modern improvements upon an unwilling populace.

The temple which served no practical purposes (as far as they could see) was neglected until the days of Herod, who was King of the Jews by the Grace of the Roman sword and whose vanity wished to renew the ancient splendor of the bygone ages. In a half-hearted manner the oppressed people set to work to obey the orders of a master who was not of their own choosing.

When the last stone had been placed in its proper position another revolution broke out against the merciless Roman tax gatherers. The temple was the first victim of this rioting. The soldiers of the Emperor Titus promptly set fire to this center of the old Jewish faith. But the city of Jerusalem was spared.

Palestine however continued to be the scene of unrest.

The Romans who were familiar with all sorts of races of men and who ruled countries where a thousand different divinities were worshipped did not know how to handle the Jews. They did not understand the Jewish character at all. Extreme tolerance (based upon indifference) was the foundation upon which Rome had constructed her very successful Empire. Roman governors never interfered with the religious belief of subject tribes. They demanded that a picture or a statue of the

Emperor be placed in the temples of the people who inhabited the outlying parts of the Roman domains. This was a mere formality and it did not have any deep significance. But to the Jews such a thing seemed highly sacrilegious and they would not desecrate their Holiest of Holies by the carven image of a Roman potentate.

They refused.

The Romans insisted.

In itself a matter of small importance, a misunderstanding of this sort was bound to grow and cause further ill-feeling. Fifty-two years after the revolt under the Emperor Titus the Jews once more rebelled. This time the Romans decided to be thorough in their work of destruction.

Jerusalem was destroyed.

The temple was burned down.

A new Roman city, called Aelia Capitolina was erected upon the ruins of the old city of Solomon.

A heathenish temple devoted to the worship of Jupiter was built upon the site where the faithful had worshipped Jehovah for almost a thousand years.

The Jews themselves were expelled from their capital and thousands of them were driven away from the home of their ancestors.

From that moment on they became wanderers upon the face of the Earth.

But the Holy Laws no longer needed the safe shelter of a royal shrine.

Their influence had long since passed beyond the narrow confines of the land of Judah. They had become a living symbol of Justice wherever honorable people tried to live a righteous life.

十四　达马士革①——经商的城市

埃及的古城已从这地球的面上不见了。尼尼微和巴比伦是尘沙和砖瓦的废墩了。耶路撒冷的古殿，昔日的光荣已逝，卧葬于黑暗的残址下了。

不过有一个城市至今还独自存留着。

它是叫作达马士革。

在它的四扇大门和坚固的城墙中，一群忙碌的人民已连绵的五千年接续着它的日常的职业，而这叫作"直的街"。这是这城的商业的要道，古往今来的人已经踏过一万五千年。

达马士革谦逊地由一亚摩利人的巩固的边城，开始它的事业，那些有名的沙漠的亚摩利人产生了大罕默刺匹王。当亚摩利人更向东迁移进了美索不达迷亚的山谷以创始巴比伦国时，达马

――――――――――

① 通译为大马士革。

士革继续着做一随那住在小亚细亚山中野性的喜泰人的商站。

在适当的时期内，这最早的居民，又被塞姆族的阿剌米亚人并吞了。然而城自己并没改变了它的属性。经过了这许多变化，它依旧保存着商业的重要的中心地。

它是位于从埃及到美索不达迷亚的要道上；它是从地中海的海口一星期以内的路程。它并没出过大将军，政治家和有名的王。它并没克服过一哩的邻近的领土，它和全世界通商，而供给商人和工匠以一安全之家。偶然它也施用它的言语于西亚细亚的大部分。

在国与国之间，行商是常需要迅速而切实的交通方法。古萨谟利亚人的精致的钉刻文的组织，于阿剌米亚的商人不免太复杂。他发明了一种新的字母，能够比巴比伦古代的锲样的图像写得更快。

阿剌米亚人的口讲的言语，是依着他们的商情的信札。

阿剌米亚语成了古世界的英吉利语；在美索不达迷亚的大半部分中，它是像土语一样地通

遥远的地平线

行。在有些国度中它确然代理了旧族语。

当耶稣于群众前讲道时，他并非用古的犹太语——那摩西尝用了解释律法给他的同道漂泊的人听的。

他讲阿剌米亚语，商人的言语，这已成了古地中海社会中的质朴的人民的言语。

XIV. DAMASCUS
—THE CITY OF TRADE

THE old cities of Egypt have disappeared from the face of the earth. Nineveh and Babylon are deserted mounds of dust and brick. The ancient temple of Jerusalem lies buried beneath the blackened ruins of its own glory.

One city alone has survived the ages.

It is called Damascus.

Within its four great gates and its strong walls a busy people has followed its daily occupations for five thousand consecutive years and the "Street called Straight" which is the city's main artery of commerce, has seen the coming and going of one hundred and fifty generations.

Humbly Damascus began its career as a fortified frontier town of the Amorites, those famous desert folk who had given birth to the great King Hammurapi. When the Amorites moved further eastward into the valley of Mesopotamia to found the Kingdom of Babylon, Damascus had been continued as a trading post with the wild Hittites who inhabited the mountains of Asia Minor.

In due course of time the earliest inhabitants had been absorbed by another Semitic tribe, called the Aramaeans. The city itself however had not changed its character. It remained throughout these many changes an important center of commerce.

It was situated upon the main road from Egypt to Mesopotamia and it was within a week's distance from the harbors on the Mediterranean. It produced no great generals and statesmen and no famous Kings. It did not conquer a single mile of neighboring territory. It traded with all the world and offered a safe home to the merchant and to the artisan. Incidentally it bestowed its language upon the greater part of western Asia.

Commerce has always demanded quick and

practical ways of communication between different nations. The elaborate system of nail-writing of the ancient Sumerians was too involved for the Aramaean business man. He invented a new alphabet which could be written much faster than the old wedge-shaped figures of Babylon.

The spoken language of the Aramaeans followed their business correspondence.

Aramaean became the English of the ancient world. In most parts of Mesopotamia it was understood as readily as the native tongue. In some countries it actually took the place of the old tribal dialect.

And when Christ preached to the multitudes, he did not use the ancient Jewish speech in which Moses had explained the Laws unto his fellow wanderers.

He spoke in Aramaean, the language of the merchant, which had become the language of the simple people of the old Mediterranean world.

十五　　航越地平线的腓尼基人

　　探险者是勇敢的人，为了他自己的好奇心，勇敢前进。

　　也许他住在高山之麓。

　　还有几千的别种人民虽也住在山麓，他们却十分知足地置山于不问。

　　这是很使得探险者不快乐的。他要知道这山里究竟隐藏了些什么神秘。一定要亲眼去看看，它的后面有否别一座山，或者一块平原？它的陡峻的悬崖是否突从海洋的黑浪升起来，还是俯瞰着沙漠？

　　晴美的一天，这真实的探险者离别了他的家族，和安适的家，出去探求。也许有一日他会回来，对他的漠不关心的亲戚诉述他的经验。也许他会被坠下的石块或是厉害的风雪所杀。那样，他绝不会回来，善良的邻人摇着他们的头，说："他得到了他所应得的。他为甚不守在家里如我们其余的人一样？”

但是这世界需要这种人，在他们已死了许多年，而别人由他们的发现已获得了利益后，他们往往接受着有相当的铭刻的雕像。

较最高的山更可惊的，是细细的远远的地平线，这似乎是世界的尽头。探险家经过了水天相接的地方，那里的一切都是黑暗的绝望和死灭。上天对于这般人是有好生之德的。

在人已造了他的第一只笨重的船以后的世世纪纪，他仍在相熟的海岸的乐景中，远离着地平线。

于是来了不知畏惧的腓尼基人，他们远远的越过视线以外的地方。突然地这被禁着的港洋变成了平安的商业的大道，而地平线的危险的威吓变成了神话。

这些腓尼基的航海者是塞姆人。他们的祖先是跟巴比伦人犹太人和一切的别种人一起住在阿剌伯的沙漠中。但是当犹太人占据巴力斯坦时，腓尼基人的城市已是几世纪的老者了。

那儿有两个腓尼基人的商业中心。

这叫作太尔，而那叫作西顿。它们是建造在

腓尼基人

高的绝壁上，据传说没有仇敌能克取它们。为美索不达迷亚的人民的利益起见，他们的船到处行驶在地中海以采集物产。

起初航海者不过航行到法兰西和西班牙的远离的海岸，跟这土人交易，而赶速带了谷类和金属回家。后来他们在沿西班牙意大利希腊和远至出有价值的锡的细黎群岛的海岸建筑了具有堡垒的商站。

对于欧罗巴的野蛮人，这种商站似乎是美丽和奢华的梦景。他们请求商站中的人允许他们住近它的城墙，以便观看许多帆船，从不可知的东方载了很讨欢喜的商品进这海口时的奇观。渐渐地他们离弃了他们的茅篷，而在腓尼基人的堡垒的周围，亲自造了小的木屋。由此，许多商站渐变成了全邻地的一切的人民的市场。

今日这种大城如马舍尔斯和加的兹是骄傲着他们的腓尼基人的根源，但是他们的元祖，太尔和西顿已经死了而且已被忘却了二千余年，腓尼基人呢，没有一个遗留着。

这是厄运，但这也是十分应该的。

并没用了多大的努力，腓尼基人是渐渐富足了，但是他们不知道怎样得当地用他们的钱财。他们从不曾留意过书籍或学问。他们只是留意金钱。

他们在全世界买卖奴隶。他们强迫着外国的移民在他们的工场内工作。只要有机会时，他们欺骗着他们的邻人，使自己被地中海的其余一切的人民所痛恨。

他们是勇敢而奋力的航海者，他们不妨诚实的交易，也可以用欺诈和狡猾的方法得到眼前的利益。每每在选择这两种手段之一时，他们便显出他们的弱点来了。因为他们是世界中能够驾驶大船唯一的水手，所以其余一切的国家都想请他们去服务。一到别人也知道怎样把舵和开船时，便立刻驱逐了这些狡诈的腓尼基的商人。

从那时起，太尔和西顿于亚细亚的商业社会上失掉了他们旧有的把持权，他们从没奖励过艺术或科学。他们知道怎样搜索这七个海，将它们的投机改变成有利益的置产。然而没有国家能安稳地建立在只有物质的基础上。

　　腓尼基地方常是一个没有灵魂的会计室。

　　它的灭亡，因为它把善藏的财宝箱，和国家最高的理想，一样的看重。

XV. THE PHOENICIANS WHO SAILED BEYOND THE HORIZON

A pioneer is a brave fellow, with the courage of his own curiosity.

Perhaps he lives at the foot of a high mountain.

So do thousands of other people. They are quite contented to leave the mountain alone.

But the pioneer feels unhappy. He wants to know what mysteries this mountain hides from his eyes. Is there another mountain behind it, or a plain? Does it suddenly arise with its steep cliffs from the dark waves of the ocean or does it overlook a desert?

One fine day the true pioneer leaves his family and the safe comfort of his home to go and find out. Perhaps he will come back and tell his experience to his indifferent relatives. Or he will be killed by falling stones or a treacherous blizzard. In that case he does not return at all and the good neighbors shake their heads and say, "He got what he deserved. Why did he not stay at home like the rest of us?"

But the world needs such men and after they have been dead for many years and others have reaped the benefits of their discoveries, they always receive a statue with a fitting inscription.

More terrifying than the highest mountain is the thin line of the distant horizon. It seems to be the end of the world itself. Heaven have mercy upon those who pass beyond this meeting-place of sky and water, where all is black despair and death.

And for centuries and centuries after man had built his first clumsy boats, he remained within the pleasant sight of one familiar shore and kept away from the horizon.

Then came the Phoenicians who knew no such fears. They passed beyond the sight of land. Suddenly the forbidding ocean was turned into a peaceful highway of commerce and the dangerous menace of the horizon became a myth.

These Phoenician navigators were Semites. Their ancestors had lived in the desert of Arabia together with the Babylonians, the Jews and all the others. But when the Jews occupied Palestine, the cities of the Phoenicians were already old with the age of many centuries.

There were two Phoenician centers of trade.

One was called Tyre and the other was called Sidon. They were built upon high cliffs and rumor had it that no enemy could take them. Far and wide their ships sailed to gather the products of the Mediterranean for the benefit of the people of Mesopotamia.

At first the sailors only visited the distant shores of France and Spain to barter with the natives and hastened home with their grain and metal. Later they had built fortified trading posts along the coasts of Spain and Italy and Greece and the far-off Scilly Islands where the valuable tin was found.

To the uncivilized savages of Europe, such a

trading post appeared as a dream of beauty and luxury. They asked to be allowed to live close to its walls, to see the wonderful sights when the boats of many sails entered the harbor, carrying the much-desired merchandise of the unknown east. Gradually they left their huts to build themselves small wooden houses around the Phoenician fortresses. In this way many a trading post had grown into a market place for all the people of the entire neighborhood.

Today such big cities as Marseilles and Cadiz are proud of their Phoenician origin, but their ancient mothers, Tyre and Sidon, have been dead and forgotten for over two thousand years and of the Phoenicians themselves, none have survived.

This is a sad fate but it was fully deserved.

The Phoenicians had grown rich without great effort, but they had not known how to use their wealth wisely. They had never cared for books or learning. They had only cared for money.

They had bought and sold slaves all over the world. They had forced the foreign immigrants to work in their factories. They cheated their neighbors whenever they had a chance and they had made themselves detested by all the other people of the Mediterranean.

They were brave and energetic navigators, but they showed themselves cowards whenever they were obliged to choose between honorable dealing and an immediate profit, obtained through fraudulent and shrewd trading.

As long as they had been the only sailors in the world who could handle large ships, all other nations had been in need of their services. As soon as the others too had learned how to handle a rudder and a set of sails, they at once got rid of the tricky Phoenician merchant.

From that moment on, Tyre and Sidon had lost their old hold upon the commercial world of Asia. They had never encouraged art or science. They had known how to explore the seven seas and turn their ventures into profitable investments. No state, however, can be safely built upon material possessions alone.

The land of Phoenicia had always been a counting-house without a soul.

It perished because it had honored a well-filled treasure chest as the highest ideal of civic pride.

十六　字母随在行商后

我已对你们说过埃及人怎样用小的图像保存言语。我已描述过楔样的记号，这给美索不达迷亚的人民用来做在家和在外的办理商业的便捷的方法。

但是我们自己的字母怎样呢？那些追随我们一生的，从我们落地时的人口证到我们丧葬时的讣闻的末一字的，坚实的小的字母是从哪里来的？它们是否埃及文巴比伦文或者阿刺米亚文，还是它们是绝然不同的东西？它们是每种文的一些些，如我现在所要告诉你们的。

以复述我们的言语为目的，我们近代的字母是一种不很完备的器具。有一天总有一个人会发明一种新的文字的组织，这会给我们的每一发音有一个它自己的小像。但是虽有它的许多不完备，我们近代的字母的语句同了它们的精密而正确的表兄弟——数码（它们从远离的印度漂流进欧罗巴时，几乎在字母第一次侵占后的十世纪）完成它们的日课，十分地精切而完全。然而这些字母的最初的历史是深深的神秘，须费许多年的刻苦的研究，我们才能解明它。

这是我们深知的——我们的字母不是突然被一个聪明的少年律法师发明的。这是几百年来从几种极老而又极复杂的组织中逐渐改进出来的。

在前一章，我已对你们说过，智慧的阿刺米亚商人的言语散遍在西亚细亚，做了国际的交通的方法。腓尼基人的言语，在他们的邻人中，总不会很通行。除了极少数的字句以外，我们不知道它是何种语言。然而他们的文字的组织是被带进了广漠的地中海的每一隅，每一腓尼基的属地成了它的更远的传递的中心点。

这是依旧还待解释的，为什么这对于艺术或科学没丝毫工作的腓尼基人，会偶然得了这种精密且便捷的文字的组织，而别的较优的国家仍忠诚地守着这古老笨拙的书写。

在一切的别件事以前，腓尼基人是实际的商人。他们并非到国外去欣赏风景。他们到欧罗巴的远隔的部分和阿非利加的更远的部分的航行，是以找寻财富为目的。在太尔和西顿中，光阴便是黄金，商业的记录用象形文或萨谟利亚文写，是徒费忙碌的书记的可贵的时间，书记是可以派做更有用的差事的。

我们的近代的商业社会中，断定这种记录口授的信札的老法子，在匆忙的近代生活是太慢了，有一聪明人发明了一种点和画的法式，它能像猎狗追赶野兔般紧追着口讲的言语。

我们称这种法式为"速写"。

腓尼基的商人做了同样的事情。

他们从埃及人的象形文借用了几个图像，并简单化了许多巴比伦人楔形的符号。

为了便利于迅速，他们牺牲了这老法式的美丽的形象，他们从前代的几千图像减少成只有廿二个简短而且便捷的字母。他们在家乡将它试用，待它证实了成功时，他们传它到国外。

在埃及文和巴比伦文中，文字是很严肃的事物——有些几乎是圣的了。有许多改善已被建议着，但是这些已被看做渎神的改革，常弃置不用。那无兴趣于敬神的腓尼基人成功了别人所已失败的。他们不能引用他们的字体于美索不达迷亚和埃及中，但是在全不知文字的艺术的地中海的人民中，腓尼基人的字母是一大成功，在那广漠的海的一切的角里，我们找到了花瓶，柱子和残迹上覆以腓尼基文的题铭。

那已迁住过爱琴海的许多岛的印度欧罗巴的希腊人立刻采取了这外国字母来做他们自己的言语。某种希腊文的发音，不熟于塞姆的腓尼基人的听官的，须用他们自己的语句。这些是被发现而增加于别的上。

但是希腊人并不便止于此。

他们改进这语言的记录的全组织。

古亚细亚的人民的一切的文字的组织有一共同点。

复述了子音，但是读者是被逼着揣摩母音。

这是没有像它的想像般困难。

那印在我们的新闻纸中的广告和布告，我们时常省略母音。新闻记者和打电报者也时常发明他们自己的言语，这废去一切的过多的母音，而只用这种置备一骨架所必须的子音，当故事重写时，母音能从骨架中插入。

但是这种不完备的文字的组织，终不能成为

通行的，希腊人用了他们的合宜的见解，加增了几个额外的符号，以重制了 "a" "e" "i" "o" 和 "u"。这已做了后，他们有了一种让他们写几乎每种语言中的每件事物的字母。

在耶稣生前的五世纪，这些字母经过了亚得里亚海而从雅典漂流到了罗马。

罗马的兵士带它们到西欧罗巴的最远的一角，并教给我们自己的祖先用这小的腓尼基人的符号。

十二世纪后，巴散丁的传教师带这字母进了黑暗的俄罗斯的平原的隐沉的荒地。

今日全世界的一半以上的人民，用这种亚细亚的字母记录着他们的思想，并保存着他们的知识的记录，以利于他们的子子孙孙。

XVI. THE ALPHABET
FOLLOWS THE TRADE

I have told you how the Egyptians preserved speech by means of little figures. I have described the wedge-shaped signs which served the people of Mesopotamia as a handy means of transacting business at home and abroad.

But how about our own alphabet? From whence came those compact little letters which follow us throughout our life, from the date on our birth certificate to the last word of our funeral notice? Are they Egyptian or Babylonian or Aramaic or are they something entirely different? They are a little bit of everything, as I shall now tell you.

Our modern alphabet is not a very satisfactory instrument for the purpose of reproducing our speech. Some day a genius will invent a new system of writing which shall give each one of our sounds a little picture of its own. But with all its many imperfections the letters of our modern alphabet perform their daily task quite nicely and fully as well as their very accurate and precise cousins, the numerals, who wandered into Europe from distant India, almost ten centuries after the first invasion of the alphabet. The earliest history of these letters, however, is a deep mystery and it will take many years of painstaking investigation before we can solve it.

This much we know—that our alphabet was not suddenly invented by a bright young scribe. It developed and grew during hundreds of years out of a number of older and more complicated systems.

In my last chapter I have told you of the language of the intelligent Aramaean traders which spread throughout western Asia, as an international means of communication. The language of the Phoenicians was never very popular among their neighbors. Except for a very few words we do not know what sort of tongue it was. Their system of writing, however, was carried into every corner of the vast Mediterranean and every Phoenician colony became a center for its further distribution.

It remains to be explained why the Phoenicians, who did nothing to further either art or science, hit upon such a compact and handy system of writing, while other and superior nations remained faithful to the old clumsy scribbling.

The Phoenicians, before all else, were practical business men. They did not travel abroad to admire the scenery. They went upon their perilous voyages to distant parts of Europe and more distant parts of Africa in search of wealth. Time was money in Tyre and Sidon and commercial documents written in hieroglyphics or Sumerian wasted useful hours of busy clerks who might be employed upon more useful errands.

When our modern business world decided that the old-fashioned way of dictating letters was too slow for the hurry of modern life, a clever man devised a simple system of dots and dashes which could follow the spoken word as closely as a hound follows a hare.

This system we call "shorthand".

The Phoenician traders did the same thing.

They borrowed a few pictures from the Egyptian hieroglyphics and simplified a number of wedge-shaped figures from the Babylonians.

They sacrificed the pretty looks of the older system for the benefit of speed and they reduced the thousands of images of the ancient world to a short and handy alphabet of only twenty-two letters. They tried it out at home and when it proved a success, they carried it abroad.

Among the Egyptians and the Babylonians, writing had been a very serious affair—something almost holy. Many improvements had been proposed but these had been invariably discarded as sacrilegious innovations. The Phoenicians who were not interested in piety succeeded where the others had failed. They could not introduce their script into

Mesopotamia and Egypt, but among the people of the Mediterranean, who were totally ignorant of the art of writing, the Phoenician alphabet was a great success and in all nooks and corners of that vast sea we find vases and pillars and ruins covered with Phoenician inscriptions.

The Indo-European Greeks who had migrated to the many islands of the Aegean Sea at once applied this foreign alphabet to their own language. Certain Greek sounds, unknown to the ears of the Semitic Phoenicians, needed letters of their own. These were invented and added to the others.

But the Greeks did not stop at this.

They improved the whole system of speech-recording.

All the systems of writing of the ancient people of Asia had one thing in common.

The consonants were reproduced but the reader was forced to guess at the vowels.

This is not as difficult as it seems.

We often omit the vowels in advertisements and in

announcements which are printed in our newspapers. Journalists and telegraph operators, too, are apt to invent languages of their own which do away with all the superfluous vowels and use only such consonants as are necessary to provide a skeleton around which the vowels can be draped when the story is rewritten.

But such an imperfect scheme of writing can never become popular, and the Greeks, with their sense of order, added a number of extra signs to reproduce the "a" and the "e" and the "i" and the "o" and the "u". When this had been done, they possessed an alphabet which allowed them to write everything in almost every language.

Five centuries before the birth of Christ these letters crossed the Adriatic and wandered from Athens to Rome.

The Roman soldiers carried them to the furthest corners of western Europe and taught our own ancestors the use of the little Phoenician signs.

Twelve centuries later, the missionaries of

Byzantine took the alphabet into the dreary wilderness of the dark Russian plain.

Today more than half of the people of the world use this Asiatic alphabet to keep a record of their thoughts and to preserve a record of their knowledge for the benefit of their children and their grandchildren.

十七　古代的终了

至此，古代的人的故事是一惊奇的事业的记录。沿尼罗河畔，在美索不达迷亚中和地中海的两岸上，人民已成就了伟大的事业，并且聪明的领袖已完成了非凡的功绩。在那里，在历史中的第一次，人已停止了做漂泊的动物。他已给他自己造了屋子村庄和广大的城市。

他已建立了国家。

他已学得了建筑和驾驶快帆船的艺术。

他已细心考察过天空，在他自己的心灵中，他已发现某种重要的道德律，这使他做了他所崇拜的神祇的同种。他已置下了一切更深的我们的知识，我们的科学，我们的艺术和那些使生活远超于孜孜然只谋食宿的基础。

一切之中最重要的，他已发明了一种记录发音的组织，这给他的子子孙孙可以知道他们祖先的经验的利益，并且可以集得这样多的知识，致他们能使自己做了自然之力的主人。

但是随着这许多功劳，古代的人有一个大失败。

他太做了习俗的奴隶了。

他并不问充足的理由。

他的理由是"在我以前，我的父亲做了如此如此的一件事情；在我的父亲前，我的祖父做了它，他们俩的遭遇是好的，所以这件事情，对我也当是好的；我一定不改变它"。他忘了这种忍耐的事实的承受，永不会提高我们，到普通的动物以上。

有一次一定有一个天才的人，拒绝了再用他的长而卷曲的尾巴的帮助从树到树的运转着（如一切的他的同族已在他以前做过的），而开始用他的脚走。

但古代的人已失了这事实的观察，而继续着用他的最初的祖先的木犁，并且继续着相信那一万年以前便被崇拜着的同样的神祇，而且还教导他的子女照样做。

代替了向前进，他站住了；这是不幸的。

有一民族新而更有力的在地平线上显现着，

这古代是灭亡了。

我们叫这些新的人民做印度欧罗巴人。像你和我，他们是白人；他们讲的言语是我们全欧罗巴人言语的同一祖先；除了匈牙利人，芬兰人和北西班牙的巴斯克人以外。

我们初次听到他们时，他们已在沿里海的两岸建着他们的家几世纪。但是有一日（这种理由我们全不知道）他们包扎了他们的所有物，置于他们所已驯养熟的马背上，他们聚集了他们的牛、狗和羊，开始漂泊着，以找寻远地的幸福和食物。其中有些迁进了中亚细亚的山中；他们好久地住在伊兰的高原之山峰间，因此他们被叫作伊兰人或雅利安人。其余的慢慢地随了西沉的太阳而占有了西欧罗巴的广漠的平原。

他们几乎跟在这书起初几页所显现了他们的形象的历史以前的人一样地不开化。但是他们是耐得住苦的种族而且是善于战斗的；他们似乎已省力地占据了这石器时代的人的猎场和草原。

他们还是十分地无知，但是谢谢侥幸的命运之神，他们是精灵的。那被地中海的商人带给他们的古代的学识，他们很迅速地采为己有。

殖民地

但是埃及巴比伦和加尔底亚的陈旧的学识，他们仅仅用来做更高和更好的事物的基石。话归本题，关于"习俗"对他们是全无意义，他们以为宇宙是他们的，考察和利用那他们所视为合宜的，乃是他们的责任，以人类的深察的知识鉴定一切的经验。

所以不久他们远越了那些古代所已认做越不过的栅栏的界限——类如心灵的月亮之山。于是他们反对着他们的前主人，在一短期内，一新而有力的文化补充了古亚细亚时代的陈旧的结构。

关于这些印度欧罗巴人和他们的企业，我将在《人类的故事》中给你们一个详细的叙述，它对你们讲到希腊人，罗马人和世界中一切的别种人。

XVII. THE END
OF THE ANCIENT WORLD

S O far, the story of ancient man has been the record of a wonderful achievement. Along the banks of the river Nile, in Mesopotamia and on the shores of the Mediterranean, people had accomplished great things and wise rulers had performed mighty deeds. There, for the first time in history, man had ceased to be a roving animal. He had built himself houses and villages and vast cities.

He had formed states.

He had learned the art of constructing and navigating swift-sailing boats.

He had explored the heavens and within his own soul he had discovered certain great moral laws which made him akin to the divinities which he worshipped. He had laid the foundations for all our further knowledge and our science and our art and those things that tended to make life sublime beyond the mere grubbing for food and lodging.

Most important of all he had devised a system of recording sound which gave unto his children and unto his children's children the benefit of their ancestors' experience and allowed them to accumulate such a store of information that they could make themselves the masters of the forces of nature.

But together with these many virtues, ancient man had one great failing.

He was too much a slave of tradition.

He did not ask enough questions.

He reasoned, "My father did such and such a thing before me and my grandfather did it before my father and they both fared well and therefore this thing ought to be good for me too and I must not change it." He forgot that this patient acceptance of facts would never have lifted us above the common herd of animals.

Once upon a time there must have been a man of genius who refused any longer to swing from tree to tree with the help of his long, curly tail (as all his people had done before him) and who began to walk on his feet.

But ancient man had lost sight of this fact and continued to use the wooden plow of his earliest ancestors and continued to believe in the same gods that had been worshipped ten thousand years before and taught his children to do likewise.

Instead of going forward he stood still and this was fatal.

For a new and more energetic race appeared upon the horizon and the ancient world was doomed.

We call these new people the Indo-Europeans. They were white men like you and me, and they spoke a language which was the common ancestor of all our European languages with the exception of Hungarian, Finnish and the Basque of Northern Spain.

When we first hear of them they had for many

centuries made their home along the banks of the Caspian Sea. But one day (for reasons which are totally unknown to us) they packed their belongings on the backs of the horses which they had trained and they gathered their cows and dogs and goats and began to wander in search of distant happiness and food. Some of them moved into the mountains of central Asia and for a long time they lived amidst the peaks of the plateau of Iran, whence they are called the Iranians or Aryans. Others slowly followed the setting sun and took possession of the vast plains of western Europe.

They were almost as uncivilized as those prehistoric men who made their appearance within the first pages of this book. But they were a hardy race and good fighters and without difficulty they seem to have occupied the hunting grounds and the pastures of the men of the stone age.

They were as yet quite ignorant but thanks to a happy Fate they were curious. The wisdom of the ancient world, which was carried to them by the traders of the Mediterranean, they very soon made their own.

But the age-old learning of Egypt and Babylonia and Chaldea they merely used as a stepping-stone to something higher and better. For "tradition", as such, meant nothing to them and they considered that the Universe was theirs to explore and to exploit as they saw fit and that it was their duty to submit all experience to the acid test of human intelligence.

Soon therefore they passed beyond those boundaries which the ancient world had accepted as impassable barriers—a sort of spiritual Mountains of the Moon. Then they turned against their former masters and within a short time a new and vigorous civilization replaced the out-worn structure of the ancient Asiatic world.

But of these Indo-Europeans and their adventures I give you a detailed account in "The Story of Mankind", which tells you about the Greeks and the Romans and all the other races in the world.

附录：与本书相关的日期①

与史前人类相关的日期这里无法提供出一些确切的数据。本书第一章出现的早期欧洲人约在5万年前就已经开始了他们的征战生涯。

埃及人

尼罗河谷地最早的文明在耶稣诞生以前，就已经发展了40个世纪。

公元前3400年，古埃及帝国成立，首都为孟斐斯。

公元前2800年至公元前2700年，埃及金字塔建成。

公元前2000年，古埃及帝国被阿拉伯牧羊人希克撒斯人摧毁。

公元前1800年，底比斯取代希克索斯，成

---

① 林徽因原译未收录该附录，此次出版为保证原著完整性增添了附录译文和原文，附录地名取现通用译名。附录译者：李云竹。

为新埃及帝国的中心。

公元前 1350 年，拉美西斯攻占东亚地区。

公元前 1300 年，犹太人离开埃及。

公元前 1000 年，埃及开始衰落。

公元前 700 年，埃及沦为古亚述国的一个行省。

公元前 650 年，埃及重获独立，建立起新的国家，定都尼罗河三角洲的赛斯。外籍人，尤其是希腊人，成为新的统治者。

公元前 525 年，埃及沦为波斯帝国的一个行省。

公元前 300 年，埃及成为一个独立的王国，由亚历山大大帝的一位将军托勒密统治。

公元前 30 年，托勒密王朝的末位公主克利欧佩特拉自尽，埃及沦为罗马帝国的一部分。

犹太人

公元前 2000 年，亚伯拉罕离开了东巴比伦的乌尔，在西亚寻找新的家园。

公元前 1550 年，犹太人占领了埃及的歌珊地。

公元前 1300 年，摩西带领犹太人逃离埃及，并为他们颁布了法律——十诫。

公元前 1250 年，犹太人跨过约旦河，占领巴勒斯坦。

公元前 1055 年，扫罗成为犹太国国王。

公元前 1025 年，大卫成为强大的犹太国国王。

公元前 1000 年，所罗门王修建了耶路撒冷圣殿。

公元前 950 年，犹太国分裂成约旦王国和以色列王国。

公元前 900 年至公元前 600 年，伟大先知时代。

公元前 722 年，亚述人攻占巴勒斯坦。

公元前 586 年，尼布甲尼撒二世攻占巴勒斯坦。出现了巴比伦之囚。

公元前 537 年，波斯国王赛勒斯允许犹太人重返巴勒斯坦。

公元前 167 年至公元前 130 年，马加比家族统治下的犹太人独立的最后阶段。

公元前 63 年，庞培将耶路撒冷纳为罗马帝国的领土。

公元前 40 年，希律王受任犹太王。

公元 70 年，罗马皇帝提图斯毁灭了耶路撒冷。

美索不达米亚

公元前 4000 年，苏美尔人占领了底格里斯河和幼发拉底河之间的土地。

公元前 2200 年，巴比伦国王汉谟拉比为子民编纂了一部著名的法典。

公元前 1900 年，亚述王国成立，定都尼尼微。

公元前 950 年至公元前 650 年，亚述统领西亚。

公元前 700 年，亚述王撒珥根攻占巴勒斯坦，埃及和阿拉伯半岛。

公元前 640 年，米堤亚反抗亚述统治。

公元前 530 年，斯基提亚人进攻亚述。王国内抗战迭起。

公元前 608 年，尼尼微毁灭，亚述从此在版图上消失。

公元前 608 年至公元前 538 年，迦勒底人重建巴比伦王国。

公元前 604 年至公元前 561 年，尼布甲尼撒二世征服耶路撒冷，占领腓尼基，巴比伦成为文明的中心。

公元前 538 年，美索不达米亚沦为波斯的一个行省。

公元前 330 年，亚历山大大帝攻占美索不达米亚。

腓尼基人

公元前 1500 年至公元前 1200 年，西顿成为腓尼基主要的贸易中心

公元前 1100 年至公元前 950 年，提尔成为腓尼基商业中心。

公元前 1000 年至公元前 600 年，腓尼基发展为殖民帝国。

公元前 850 年，迦太基成立。

公元前 586 年至公元前 573 年，尼布甲尼撒进攻提尔，提尔城毁灭。

公元前 538 年，腓尼基沦为波斯的一个行省。

公元前 60 年，腓尼基被纳入罗马帝国。

波斯人

不知从何时起，印欧人开始向欧洲和印度

进发。

公元前 1000 年通常
被称作是查拉图斯特拉时
代，这位伟大的波斯人的
先师编纂了一部杰出的德
教圣典。

公元前 650 年，印欧
米堤亚人在巴比伦王国东
部边陲发现了一个国家。

波斯塔庙

公元前 550 年至公元前 330 年，波斯帝国统
治时期，印欧人和闪族人的斗争开始。

公元前 525 年，波斯国王冈比西斯夺取埃及。

公元前 520 年至公元前 485 年，波斯国王大
流士占领巴比伦并进攻希腊。

公元前 485 年至公元前 465 年，薛西斯王试
图在东欧建立自己的政权，但以失败告终。

公元前 330 年，希腊亚历山大大帝攻克西亚
和埃及全境，波斯沦为希腊的一个行省。

闪族人统治的古老世界延续了近 40 个世
纪，基督诞生前的第四个世纪，在古老的岁月中
消亡。

印欧人曾攻占欧洲，西亚和埃及人成为印欧人的先师。

在耶稣诞生前的第四个世纪，印欧学生凌驾于西亚和埃及先师之上，以便开始进攻世界的计划。

公元前 330 年，著名的亚历山大大帝远征结束了埃及文明和美索不达米亚文明，建立起古希腊文化（欧洲文明前身）的无上权威。

APPENDIX: A FEW DATES CONNECTED WITH THE PEOPLE OF THE ANCIENT WORLD

I can not give you any positive dates connected with Prehistoric Man. The early Europeans who appear in the first chapters of this book began their career about fifty thousand years ago.

THE EGYPTIANS

The earliest civilization in the Nile Valley developed forty centuries before the birth of Christ.

3400 B.C. The Old Egyptian Empire is founded. Memphis is the capital.

2800—2700 B.C. The Pyramids are built.

2000 B.C. The Old Empire is destroyed by the Arab shepherds, called the "Hyksos".

1800 B.C. Thebes delivers Egypt from the Hyksos

and becomes the center of the New Egyptian Empire.

1350 B.C. King Rameses conquers Eastern Asia.

1300 B.C. The Jews leave Egypt.

1000 B.C. Egypt begins to decline.

700 B.C. Egypt becomes an Assyrian province.

650 B.C. Egypt regains her independence and a new State is founded with Sais in the Delta as its capital. Foreigners, especially Greeks, begin to dominate the country.

525 B.C. Egypt becomes a Persian province.

300 B.C. Egypt becomes an independent Kingdom ruled by one of Alexander the Great's generals, called Ptolemy.

30 B.C. Cleopatra, the last princess of the Ptolemy dynasty, kills herself and Egypt becomes part of the Roman Empire.

THE JEWS

2000 B.C. Abraham moves away from the land of Ur in eastern Babylonia and looks for a new home in the western part of Asia.

1550 B.C. The Jews occupy the land of Goshen in

Egypt.

1300 B.C. Moses leads the Jews out of Egypt and gives them the Law.

1250 B.C. The Jews have crossed the river Jordan and have occupied Palestine.

1055 B.C. Saul is King of the Jews.

1025 B.C. David is King of a powerful Jewish state.

1000 B.C. Solomon builds the Great Temple of Jerusalem.

950 B.C. The Jewish state is divided into two Kingdoms, that of Judah and that of Israel.

900—600 B.C. The age of the great Prophets.

722 B.C. The Assyrians conquer Palestine.

586 B.C. Nebuchadnezzar conquers Palestine. The Babylonian captivity.

537 B.C. Cyrus, King of the Persians, allows the Jews to return to Palestine.

167—130 B.C. Last period of Jewish independence under the Maccabees.

63 B.C. Pompeius makes Palestine part of the

Roman Empire.

40 B.C. Herod King of the Jews.

70 A.D. The Emperor Titus destroys Jerusalem.

MESOPOTAMIA

4000 B.C. The Sumerians take possession of the land between the Tigris and the Euphrates.

2200 B.C. Hammurapi, King of Babylon, gives his people a famous code of law.

1900 B.C. Beginning of the Assyrian State, with Nineveh as its capital.

950—650 B.C. Assyria becomes the master of western Asia.

700 B.C. Sargon, the ruler of the Assyrians, conquers Palestine, Egypt and Arabia.

640 B.C. The Medes revolt against the Assyrian rule.

530 B.C. The Scythians attack Assyria. There are revolutions all over the Kingdom.

608 B.C. Nineveh is destroyed. Assyria disappears from the map.

608—538 B.C. The Chaldeans reestablish the

Babylonian Kingdom.

604—561 B.C. Nebuchadnezzar destroys Jerusalem, takes Phoenicia and makes Babylon the center of civilization.

538 B.C. Mesopotamia becomes a Persian province.

330 B.C. Alexander the Great conquers Mesopotamia.

THE PHOENICIANS

1500—1200 B.C. The city of Sidon is the chief Phoenician center of trade.

1100—950 B.C. Tyre becomes the commercial center of Phoenicia.

1000—600 B.C. Development of the Phoenician colonial Empire.

850 B.C. Carthage is founded.

586—573 B.C. Siege of Tyre by Nebuchadnezzar. The city is captured and destroyed.

538 B.C. Phoenicia becomes a Persian province.

64 B.C. Phoenicia becomes part of the Roman Empire.

THE PERSIANS

At an unknown date the Indo-European people began their march into Europe and into India.

The year 1000 B.C. is usually given for Zarathustra, the great teacher of the Persians, who gave an excellent moral law.

650 B.C. The Indo-European Medes found

a state along the eastern boundaries

of Babylonia.

550—330 B.C. The Kingdom of the Persians. Beginning of the struggle between Indo-Europeans and Semites.

525 B.C. Cambyses, King of the Persians, takes Egypt.

520—485 B.C. Rule of Darius, King of the Persians, who conquers Babylon and attacks Greece.

485—465 B.C. Rule of King Xerxes, who tries to establish himself in eastern Europe but fails.

330 B.C. The Greek, Alexander the Great, conquers all of western Asia and Egypt and Persia becomes a Greek Province.

The ancient world which was dominated by Semitic peoples lasted almost forty centuries. In the fourth century before the birth of Christ it died of old age.

Western Asia and Egypt had been the teachers of the Indo-Europeans who had occupied Europe at an unknown date.

In the fourth century before Christ, the Indo-European pupils had so far surpassed their teachers that they could begin their conquest of the world.

The famous expedition of Alexander the Great in 330 B.C. made an end to the civilizations of Egypt and Mesopotamia and established the supremacy of Greek (that is European) culture.